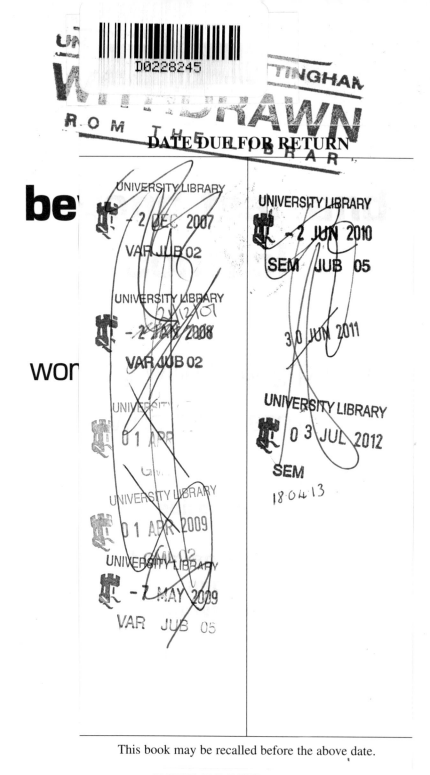

be

wor

This book may be recalled before the above date.

PCCS BOOKS
Ross-on-Wye

First published in 2007

PCCS BOOKS Ltd
2 Cropper Row
Alton Rd
Ross-on-Wye
Herefordshire
HR9 5LA
UK
Tel +44 (0)1989 763 900
www.pccs-books.co.uk

Beyond Fear and Control:
Working with young people who self-harm

A CIP catalogue record for this book is available from the British Library

ISBN 978 1 898 05987 5

Cover artwork by Lanni Gaynor

Cover design by Old Dog Graphics

Printed by Cromwell Press, Trowbridge, UK

CONTENTS

Erratum

Figure 1 on p. 93 should be as below. Please accept our apologies for any inconvenience caused.

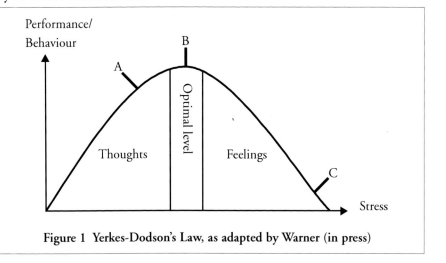

Figure 1 Yerkes-Dodson's Law, as adapted by Warner (in press)

1004965509

DEDICATION

To Miles, silent editor, now noisy contributor, born 6th December 2006.

ACKNOWLEDGMENTS

We appreciate the patience, understanding and hard work of everyone involved in the long process of putting this book together. We would especially like to thank everyone who contributed chapters. We would also like to thank workers and ex-workers at 42nd Street, especially Vera Martins (who, as the representative of 42nd Street has been hugely supportive of this book) and Mark Needham (who first had the idea to put this book together). Finally, we are extremely grateful to the young people who have contributed directly and indirectly to this book—by sharing their time, experiences and ideas with us.

FOREWORD BY
42ND STREET

42nd Street is a community-based resource for young people, aged from 13 to 25 years old, who are under stress. We are based in Greater Manchester, a socially, culturally and economically diverse area. As an organisation we have a working commitment to delivering services to young people from a wide range of backgrounds, particularly those who are socially excluded, disadvantaged and experience discrimination in their daily lives. For example, through targeted projects we work hard to make our services accessible to black young people, young women, lesbian, gay, bisexual and transgendered young people, young people questioning their sexuality and disabled young people.

Many of the young people who use our services have experienced abuse and trauma, and often use self-harm as a way to survive these experiences. Using self-harm as a survival strategy is not unique to any particular groups or communities but is found across all groups who experience abuse, oppression and discrimination. Differences may arise in the particular ways that self-harm is carried out, and this could reflect the diverse life experiences of young people and their particular experiences of oppression.

A key factor in ensuring our service is accessible to the diverse group of young people we work with has been the adoption of a young-person-centred approach. We start from the premise that young people are experts on their own experience, and that it is through taking seriously what young people tell us about their experiences that we can develop better services and practices to meet their needs. What is even more significant is that we try and work with young people holistically where nurturing identity and a sense of self is central to our practice. We are committed to sharing this approach with others, and as such we have a long history of documenting and publishing our work (42nd Street, 1983; McDermott, 1986; Davies, 2000).

It is in this context that we commissioned *Beyond Fear and Control* in order to demonstrate the benefits of working in a young-person-centred way around the specific issue of self-harm. Our aim is to provide a platform for sharing good practice that engages with experiences of oppression and discrimination but more importantly challenges the orthodoxy and thus extends the debate on working with self-harm.

42nd Street has long been aware that self-harm is a major issue for services working with young people under stress. We know this because self-harm has been one of the difficulties most frequently presented by young people who use 42nd Street. Very often it takes months of engagement before young people open up and admit to self-harm. The young people we see do not simply self-harm because it a fashion or craze or just indicative of 'growing pains' but rather as a consequence of the context in which they live. This context is getting harder for many young people who are increasingly living in a society that is ever more hostile. One of the problems in contemporary society is that young people are often seen as 'bad' rather than in need. In Manchester for example, we have witnessed a rapid growth in the use and impact of 'anti social behaviour orders' (ASBOs). These orders may be used to restrict people's actions and have been particularly targeted at young people. People may be imprisoned if they are in breech of these orders even when they have committed no actual criminal offence. Young people need affirmation, support and protection rather than condemnation and punishment (as reflected in the use of ASBOs). Young people in trouble are also young people who have often experienced abuse, bullying and social marginalisation. Young people in general are also under tremendous pressure to compete and achieve in an increasingly consumer-driven society.

It is perhaps no wonder that some young people end up using self-harm to cope with difficulties in their day-to-day lives. Over the years we have developed a good reputation for our work with young people who self-harm, and have become one of the leading voices in championing their views and needs. However, we are only too aware that we have undergone a steep learning curve in respect of self-harm that has been both challenging and provocative. We are indebted to the young people who have shared with us their experiences of, and understandings about, self-harm.

In 1995, precisely because self-harm was such a big issue for the young people who used 42nd Street, we established a dedicated suicide and self-harm project. This project sought to understand self-harm from young people's perspective, and led to the publication of *Who's Hurting Who?* (Spandler, 1996). This book demonstrated that self-harm can have a range of positive functions for the young people who do it. This was a radical argument to make at the time because it challenged fundamental assumptions in mainstream mental health that self-harm is essentially destructive and needs to be stopped.

Once this argument had been made, new approaches had to be developed to accommodate this. For example, the use of 'no self-harm' contracts was challenged. Young people specifically argued that such contracts undermined their ability to take control of their lives. At that time 42nd Street did use contractual agreements with young people, in which a young person would agree to desist from self-harming behaviour whilst receiving support from the project. After some anxious debate, the use of contracts was dropped as a therapeutic tool and replaced by a range of individual counselling, group work and informal support relationships based explicitly on the young person's own understanding of their self-harming behaviour.

The controversial nature of these actions, and the danger of them being misunderstood by the wider public, was particularly evident during the press launch for *Who's Hurting Who?* During that launch, a story was touted around the tabloid press with the headline '*voluntary sector encourages people to self-harm*', and a psychiatrist, on local television, indicated that we were out of our depth. Following this publicity, we also learnt that some services mistakenly believed that 42nd Street had 'cutting rooms.' Accepting that self-harm may be 'functional' for some young people at particular times in their lives did not mean that we actively endorsed or encouraged self-harm, nor provided places where young people could 'cut up'. Despite these misunderstandings and attempts to undermine our work, we knew from our experience that young people responded positively to a less controlling approach. We were not alone in this argument. Throughout the country, service users and progressive mental health workers were increasingly expressing dissatisfaction with traditional mental health approaches to self-harm, and advocating alternative approaches.

In 42nd Street, the suicide and self-harm project allowed us to take our first steps towards establishing a service which explicitly moved from managing or stopping self-harm, to working with young people in more permissive, person-centred and empowering ways. Some of the things it did included running groups for young people who self-harm; working closely with local accident and emergency departments to promote greater understanding; and developing and delivering training packages for practitioners. Recently, for example, we commissioned a visual arts consultancy ('box of frogs') through funding from the Camelot Foundation to develop a training package alongside young people who self-harm. The real involvement of young people who self-harm was the foundation of this piece of work. Through the creation of a character called 'Alex' through whom they could articulate their collective experiences, the work culminated in an art exhibition, live forum theatre and training package designed and delivered by young people. In addition, one of the young people involved in the work wrote a booklet about her experiences, simply trying to tell it 'the way it is' (Alex, 2006).

Our work around self-harm has gradually evolved from being a specialist issue with its own distinct service to becoming more integrated within the overall work of 42nd Street. Bringing self-harm into the mainstream of practice helps stop specialist workers and young people being isolated, overwhelmed, and solely defined by self-harm because it encourages a more holistic approach. Our aim, in commissioning this book, is to encourage more services to adopt a young-person-centred approach that empowers service users, and also supports those that work with them.

We are encouraged to know that 42nd Street is part of a growing network of individuals and services who think that working alongside young people is more important, and more effective, than trying to stop their self-harm. The people who write in this book share these values and ethics, and this book demonstrates that there is now a wide body of knowledge and evidence base that supports this type of approach. We have been inspired by young people, and hope that, in turn, this book helps support, enable and inspire better practices with young people who self-harm.

Maryam Arbabi (Community Mental Health Manager at 42nd Street)
Alistair Cox (former Co-ordinator of 42nd Street)
Vera Martins (Director of 42nd Street)

REFERENCES

Alex (2006) *In and Out of Harm's Way,* Manchester: 42nd Street.

Davies, B (2000) *StreetCred? Values and dilemmas of mental health work with young people.* Leicester: Youth Work Press.

42nd Street (1983) *Reflected Images: Self-portraits of distress.* Manchester: Youth Development Trust.

McDermott, A (1986) *Principles into Practice.* Manchester: 42nd Street.

Spandler, H (1996) *Who's Hurting Who? Young people, self-harm and suicide.* Manchester: 42nd Street.

INTRODUCTION

HELEN SPANDLER AND SAM WARNER

People harm themselves in many ways and for many different reasons. Whilst we recognise that there is a complex relationship between self-harm and suicide, this book is about supporting young people who use self-harm primarily as a way of coping with distress. In this context self-harm can be viewed as: the expression of, and temporary relief from overwhelming, unbearable and often conflicting emotions, thoughts or memories, through a self-injurious act which they can control and regulate. Undoubtedly young people who self-harm arouse strong emotional reactions in most people including fear, helplessness, confusion and anger. Responses are often based on a need to try and protect or rescue young people from danger. However, our heightened emotional response, coupled with myths and misunderstandings about both young people *and* self-harm, can lead us to respond in ways that, rather than being empowering and helpful, can be felt as controlling and harmful.

As the title *Beyond Fear and Control* suggests, this book aims to move services away from responses based on fear and assumptions that we need to manage and control young people who self-harm. It discusses ways in which services can change the focus from managing or 'stopping' self-harm to working with young people in more permissive, 'young-person-centred' and empowering ways. Although the need for such a change is increasingly being recognised, the practical implications and ethical dilemmas of this shift have rarely been explored. This book addresses this gap by providing in-depth descriptions of a range of innovative practices, which we believe can be effective in supporting young people who self-harm.

Young people have powerfully informed us how self-harm can be a valuable 'multi-purpose coping mechanism' at crucial times in their lives. However, people who self-harm also recognise that it is a way of coping with overwhelming feelings, thoughts and experiences that they would rather not have. It is essentially a 'trade-off' between damage and preservation (Warner, 2000). Young people are clear that they need support which doesn't criticise or dismantle their carefully developed coping strategies, but helps them to remain in control.

Unfortunately, service responses to self-harm frequently take control away from the individual, inadvertently leading to the young person feeling more hurt by the very people who were supposed to help them. Negative professional responses can mirror difficulties expressed by the self-harmer by joining in with the attack on the self through criticism and punishment. This results in a style of 'helping relationships' based more on power and control rather than on empathy and exploration (Norton & Dolan, 1996). In this way, interventions can be experienced as infantilising and patronising. This may ultimately reinforce the feelings which may have given rise to self-harm in the first place. This was one of the reasons why the 42nd Street research with young people was called *'Who's Hurting Who?'* (Spandler, 1996). It posed the question: if young people tell us that self-harm is sometimes a positive option available to them, and if we are to work in a 'young-person-centred' way, how could we support them without further contributing to their hurt?

Because self-harm generates considerable anxiety, endorsing the view that self-harm can, at certain times, perform important functions in people's lives, this has been a considerable challenge. Despite the fact that this type of approach has generated many positive responses from service users and providers, many organisations promoting such approaches have often been heavily criticised or misunderstood (see the Foreword to this book from 42nd Street). Criticisms suggested that this approach might be irresponsible. Changing the focus from stopping self-harm to understanding its functions may lead to a 'self-harm epidemic', ultimately resulting in increased rates of suicide. Yet for young people (and others), it is precisely the ability to exert control in their lives that reduces suicide risk. Being controlled, and having their views invalidated and ignored (whether by carers, friends or professionals) actually increases risk. Similar misunderstandings have accompanied the call to support strategies for 'harm minimisation'. Some services have mistakenly assumed that such an approach is merely a case of giving self-harmers clean razor blades (Pembroke, 2006). It is such misunderstandings that may actually prove to be harmful. Harm minimisation is a practical approach that has been promoted by survivor activists (and their allies) for a number of years and this approach is beginning to be recognised in medical and professional arenas. Despite increasing recognition of the need for new approaches, their widespread acceptance and adoption may be limited by constraints on what we consider to be 'evidence'.

THE RELATIONSHIP BETWEEN 'EVIDENCE' AND PRACTICE

Self-harm and suicide are key areas of concern for service providers in both statutory and voluntary service contexts. This is because self-harm is widespread amongst service users in most mental health and social care populations, in both community and detained settings, and across all age and social groupings (Hawton & van Heeringen, 2000). The Government has responded to this by supporting research into self-harm and suicide, and by enabling the development of policy and practices to cater for people who self-harm (Department of Health, 2001, 2002, 2003; NICE, 2004). In 2006 the Mental Health Foundation (MHF) also produced a comprehensive national inquiry into young people and self-harm (MHF, 2006).

This national inquiry is to be welcomed as it also takes seriously the concerns of young people. It takes on board their desire for greater user-centred support, more harm minimisation approaches and the recognition of self-harm as a coping strategy. In particular, it highlighted the valuable role of self-help groups in providing support to young people who self-harm (Smith & Clarke, 2003). However, whether this will result in greater investment in such support networks remains to be seen. Rather it seems likely that the search for the elusive therapeutic 'technique' may prove more seductive and lucrative.

Despite recognising that there is little 'evidence' to support specific psychological, psychiatric or pharmacological treatments (Fox & Hawton, 2004; Derouin & Bravender, 2004), the inquiry was still intent on identifying some effective 'treatment regimes' for young people who self-harm (MHF, 2006). For example, it recommended the further investigation of dialectical behaviour therapy (DBT) as a model that shows 'promising results' (in research terms), yet which service users seldom like (in practical terms). DBT was first rolled out in secure mental health contexts and is now increasingly found in child and adolescent mental health services. As Warner (2004) has discussed elsewhere, it was specifically developed to address the 'deficient' emotional modulation skills and 'suicidal' behaviour that is commonly associated with the diagnosis of borderline personality disorder. According to this model, people misunderstand their emotions (for example believing that 'everyone is untrustworthy') and their self-harming behaviour is reinforced by the environments in which they live and receive care (i.e. they gain attention). Such treatment aims to increase their emotional knowledge and to change the environment so that it is no longer reinforcing of self-harm (see Warner, 2004).

As this book confirms, self-harm has more varied functions than this model presumes. It is little wonder that it is frequently disliked by many people who self-harm. This is because it is relentlessly 'here-and-now' focused (so past abuse, for example, can be avoided and not talked about) and can be punitive (if the client self-injures the therapist will cancel the subsequent therapy session so as not to 'reinforce' the self-harming behaviour). By contrast, this model has proved to be very popular with mental health professionals: the 'here-and-now' focus means issues of abuse can be avoided, and cancelling therapy sessions legitimises therapists' feelings of hurt and anger when their clients self-injure. Just because it is a method that is easy to follow, whose outcomes (cessation of self-harm) are easy to measure, it should not restrict access to other alternative services. Whilst DBT may be helpful for some people in some circumstances, one model seldom fits all.

As the above example demonstrates, with any research or systematic review, results are dependent on the questions asked and the outcomes desired, and these may differ considerably between service providers and service users. Yet in formal evaluations of interventions, assumptions about the 'right' method and outcomes are rarely made explicit. The mantra of 'evidence-based practice' may be a step forward in relation to moving services away from professional assumptions of what works rather than what is best for clients (Pope, 2003). However, this approach still prioritises interventions which have simple goals that are amenable to formal measurement (and so can be 'proved', like DBT), and are short term (and hence, economical) in focus. Furthermore, such approaches tend to 'fix' clients' assumed goals into strictly defined categories of (individual) problems and leave little room for manoeuvrable goals or self-definition (Parker, 2007). It is for these reasons that cognitive behavioural forms of psychotherapy predominate in the National Health Service. Hence, too narrow an approach to defining 'best evidence' can lead to the latest model being imposed uncritically on the individual, regardless of his/her own circumstances and choices (Pembroke, 2006). This means that despite current policy directives emphasising 'individual choice', the growth of a too narrowly defined evidence-based approach may limit service options in the future—especially if the 'best evidence' doesn't seem to support the service option the service user prefers.

Not only is this ideal of evidence-based practice often limited and impractical, but the hierarchy of evidence credibility effectively dismisses practices that are not considered amenable to scientific technological testing (Humphries, 2003; Burton & Chapman, 2004; Webb, 2001). Moreover, policy and legislation often owe more to prevailing ideological and economic concerns than to rational thinking and available data. Under pressure from political and cultural concerns, policy decisions and practices in mental health tend to fall back on coercive measures for which there is little or no 'evidence' (Cooper, 2003).

Of course we need to know the impact and outcomes of various interventions in order to provide services that do more good than harm. However, this kind of evidence-based approach has less interest in values, processes or quality of relationships. Instead it tends to focus on particular clinical models of interventions and contains pre-existing assumptions of what 'good outcomes' might be. In particular, outcome-focused research can be very problematic in any mental health research where the desired outcomes are often unclear and contested. This is particularly highlighted in self-harm. Here, research tends to prioritise outcomes relating to 'symptoms' (for example, either stopping or lessened self-harm) whereas survivors may personally focus on improvements in other aspects of their lives. Therefore, such an approach can sideline the needs and views of service users. This was one of the reasons the two 'experts by experience' resigned from the steering group of the panel for the development of the Department of Health guidelines on the treatment of self-harm (NICE, 2004; Smith & Pembroke, 2005). This panel was unable to view the perspectives and testimonies of survivors, or examples of 'good practice', as anything more than the bottom level of the 'evidence hierarchy'.

The approach we have adopted in this book is to prioritise 'practice-based evidence' and to provide a platform for the development of 'critical best practices' (Ferguson, 2003). Such approaches are rooted in practice and are able to understand the messy and contradictory realities practitioners often face (Burton & Chapman, 2004). The focus shifts from which technique is best for this problem to what underlying principles are associated with individually defined 'best outcomes'. This move from technique to principle means that a much wider understanding of 'what works' can be applied and evaluated. Accordingly this book offers 'evidence' for a range of alternative approaches to working with young people. Although the methods and focus of work changes, the underlying principles remain consistent. Hence, this book offers a body of evidence that supports a specific way of thinking through how we work with young people and self-harm. It does not prescribe any particular method—as different ways of working will be appropriate for different young people in different situations and maybe at different times in their lives. The evidence base that this book provides, therefore, is about a specific value base (rather than technique or method). This value base has developed out of dissatisfaction with dominant mental health practices, and is rooted in the recent history of abuse/self-harm/psychiatric survivor movements.

OUR EVIDENCE BASE: REPLACING TECHNIQUES
WITH PRINCIPLES

This book is situated within a wider radical history of innovative practice and critique.

A self-harm survivors' movement began to take shape in the early 1990s in the UK and was directly influenced by the wider psychiatric survivor movement and feminism (Cresswell, 2005). Women who have survived abuse and people (primarily women) who have survived psychiatry began to organise their own voice in relation to self-harm. For example, in 1989, psychiatric survivors from the organisation Survivors Speak Out (SSO) and feminist activists from the Bristol Crisis Service for Women (BCSW) put together the first national conference organised by self-harmers themselves (Asylum, 1989). Such initiatives resulted in a number of important publications such as *Self-harm: Perspectives from personal experience* (Pembroke, 1994) and various publications from the Bristol Crisis Service for Women (Arnold, 1995), and later the Basement Project (Arnold & Magill, 1997; Babiker & Arnold, 1998) and Action Consultancy Training (Lefevre, 1996). This movement based its existence on challenging psychiatric myths and misconceptions about self-harm and has been critical of conventional psychiatric interventions as well as traditional forms of psychotherapy. This ultimately culminated in the setting up of the National Self Harm Network in 1995 and, since then, increasing numbers of local and national self-harm support and self-help groups have been established. As a result, a critique of psychiatric and psychological interventions around self-harm has gathered pace and alternative, more permissive approaches have been increasingly recognised and practiced. Some of this progressive thinking has gone on to influence policy and practice. It is clear that progress has been made with the support both of prominent survivor activists as well as particular progressive professionals and workers, some of whom have contributed to this book.

This book brings together workers and activists who have been part of, or influenced by, this growing movement. As noted, although the chapters in this book reflect a wide range of practices they still share key values and principles. First, all the chapters have a clear understanding of the social roots of distress and the importance of the role of oppression and powerlessness in the experience of self-harm. Because self-harm is associated with abuse, oppression, discrimination and attendant feelings of powerlessness and alienation, it is unsurprising that self-harm is particularly common in marginalised groups of young people. These include young people from black and minoritised ethnic communities, lesbian, gay, bisexual or transgendered young people and young people with disabilities (SDC & RUHBC, 2005).

Taking their experiences seriously is the cornerstone to all the contributions in this book. Most of the approaches set out in this book are not only relevant to marginalised groups of young people, but are practices which have developed in response to, and alongside, their concerns. What we have tried to do, in presenting the range of approaches described in the book, is to demonstrate how our shared value base can inform different ways of working, with a range of young people. Hence although some chapters broadly focus on young women, young men or black young people, we have deliberately avoided having chapters that focus too specifically on distinct groups of marginalised young people because we do not want to suggest that a particular method, focus or technique can only be used with a particular group. Rather, our intention is to demonstrate that a value base which is directly concerned with abuse and oppression has much to offer marginalised young people.

The second principle that informs our approach is that we believe it is crucial to make a distinction between self-harm and attempted suicide. This is not to deny any overlap between the two, as there are many emotional similarities between feelings associated with self-harm and suicide. However, we are making a distinction between acts of self-harm which are intended as a coping strategy and self-harm as a means of ending life. If we do not make this distinction in practice then potentially all self-harm could be treated as attempted suicide or 'para suicide' resulting in more controlling and risk-aversive practices. Conversely, if we primarily view attempted suicide as a form of self-harm we may fail to distinguish situations that may be life threatening.

The third principle arises out of making this distinction. As noted, the focus of this book is on self-harm as a coping strategy, and hence part of the value base that underpins our different practices is that the focus of intervention should not be assumed to be primarily about stopping self-harm at the expense of other considerations. Rather, our aim is to be young-person focused (the fourth principle). That is, our aim is to enable young people to set their own aims, goals and agendas and, hence, to ensure young people who self-harm are able to remain in control of their lives as far as possible.

Our fifth and final principle relates to those that work with, and care for, young people who self-harm. If we are to develop practices that are permissive and enabling, then it is crucial that we are supported to work in this way. This means having explicit support from services. This may include having clear guidelines and policies in respect of self-harm, abuse, oppression and marginalisation. It also means having access to ongoing support and supervision. If workers are to be able to take responsibility for their own feelings and reactions to self-harm, rather than project these feelings on to the young people, they need an opportunity to reflect on the work they do.

Even though these principles inform all our ways of working, they do not result in a narrow set of practices. Rather, there is much scope for creative differences and distinctions in emphasis and focus when working with young people who self-harm. For example, some chapters in this book focus on working alongside young people who use self-harm as a coping strategy and discuss supporting them directly around harm minimisation strategies. Others focus more on working with young people on some of the issues underlying self-harm, such as abuse and neglect. The appropriateness of these responses depends on the context and relationship, and especially the (often changing) needs of the young person. For example, in Chapter 5, Rose demonstrates how keeping quiet worked for her client, whilst in Chapter 6 Theres demonstrates the benefits of a more active approach. In addition, harm minimisation may be an appropriate strategy in some circumstances (as both Louise Pembroke and Clare and Terri Shaw argue in this book). However, if approached insensitively, this approach could merely reinforce a young person's feeling that they are only worthy of further harm. These examples highlight the problem of any approach being applied uncritically. They also demonstrate that there is not one method or technique that can be applied across the board in all circumstances.

The chapters are varied in style and content, and this reflects the different types of work that contributors are involved in. Whilst not exhaustive, these contributions cover a wide range of approaches from counselling, social action, youth work, research, law, policy and activism. Although we have made a concerted attempt to make chapters accessible, some of these chapters are still 'hard' reading. This is necessary because of the issue that is the subject of this book. We do not want to romanticise self-harm, nor do we wish to encourage voyeurism, but we do want to offer knowledge and information that will help us develop a greater understanding of some of the issues involved in supporting young people effectively. In order to achieve this aim, the chapters are organised into three sections.

OUTLINE OF CHAPTERS

Part One: Working alongside Young People
In order to move 'beyond fear and control', we need to work alongside young people and develop supportive relationships and services that respond to their needs in ways that are acceptable to them. If we don't do this, we will continue to offer help or treatment that is considered harmful by the young person seeking support. This vicious circle of harm created through inadequate

service responses is powerfully evoked in Chapter 1 by Clare and Terri Shaw. Clare describes how her self-harm escalated dramatically whilst an in-patient on various psychiatric wards. She demonstrates the negative impact of continued misunderstandings of her self-harm on both herself and her family. However, it is also *A Dialogue of Hope and Survival* as they demonstrate how working alongside Clare with the support of family and friends can be effective.

The following three chapters describe how the principles of working alongside young people might translate into more work-based settings. Eamonn Kirk's and Keith Green's chapters are both based on reflections of work carried out at the 42nd Street project in Manchester. In Chapter 2, *Edges and Ledges*, Eamonn explores the value of developing informal support relationships with young people using a variety of approaches developed from youth work and social work. As noted earlier, one of the anxieties that service providers have about a more permissive and 'collective' approach to self-harm is the fear of 'contagion' and a particular concern that if young people meet together they might encourage each other to harm themselves. Contrary to this fear a number of group-work approaches have been effectively used with young people who self-harm. In Chapter 3, *Finding your own Voice*, Keith Green introduces a particular type of group-work approach based on a 'social action' model of change. This approach assumes that young people can be supported to make active challenges to the social context which contributes to their distress. Finally, in Chapter 4, *Supportive Communities and Helpful Practices: The challenge for services*, Ian Murray discusses working alongside two young women in a residential setting and explores the essential qualities of developing helpful relationships. Out of his experience, Ian lays out the key challenges for service providers and commissioners in providing more adequate and responsive services to young people who self-harm.

PART TWO: ABUSE, OPPRESSION AND SELF-HARM

Self-harm tends to occur in the context of past (and present) abusive and neglectful social relationships. Despite this, there is little acknowledgement of the impact of experiences of discrimination, oppression and inequalities on self-injury (SDC & RUHBC, 2005). Whilst the national inquiry into young people and self-harm minimised a focus on power and abuse, this section explicitly explores the social roots of distress. It highlights both the impact of sexual abuse, oppression and racism, as well as drawing attention to the ways in which mental health services (and the wider society) can compound young people's hurt by undermining their coping strategies, pathologising their distress and misunderstanding their experiences. Thus Part Two explicitly focuses on the use (and misuse) of power.

In Chapter 5, *Calming Down: Self-injury as stress control*, Rose Cameron looks at how early childhood experiences of neglect and abuse can undermine young people's ability to self-soothe during periods of distress. Rose provides a detailed account of the possible neurological, biochemical and psychological evidence base to our claim that self-harm may be functional for some people. Rose introduces the notion of people dissociating from painful experiences and, in Chapter 6, Theres Fickl explores this theme further through an in-depth discussion of working with young people who self-harm who also dissociate in the context of past abuse. Specifically, Theres raises the question, *Whose Fear Is It Anyway?*, as she demonstrates how workers' own fears and dissociative coping strategies can inhibit their ability to develop genuine therapeutic relationships with young people who self-harm. She demonstrates the importance of good supervision and support for workers in being able to recognise how their own fear can impact on their work.

Taking this discussion onto broader territory, in Chapter 7, *Disordered Boundaries: A critique of 'Borderline Personality Disorder'*, Gillian Proctor highlights how (young) women's experiences of abuse and violence can be hidden and/or pathologised through traditional medical and psychiatric conceptualisations of mental illness, particularly through the category 'Borderline Personality Disorder'. Gillian provides an important critique of this psychiatric label and offers some insights in developing therapeutic relationships based more on equality and mutuality to counteract the abusive and/or neglectful experiences many girls and young women have experienced in society.

It is not only psychiatric abuse or familial abuse that impacts on young people's distress. There are also a variety of ways that ongoing wider social oppression adversely effects mental health and contributes to self-harm. Whilst there is some acceptance of the possible links between sexual abuse and self-harm, there is less understanding of the impact of other forms of abuse and oppression on young people's self-harm. In Chapter 8, *'To that piece of each of us that refuses to be silent'*, Vera Martins looks at the impact of racism and examines her experience of supporting two young people who specifically attacked parts of their black identity through their use of self-harm. Vera explores how issues of identity formation can be addressed while working with oppressed young people who self-harm.

PART THREE: STRATEGIES OF SURVIVAL

In the broader context outlined in the previous section, it may seem difficult to work in progressive ways to effectively support young people who self-harm. If the wider society (family, psychiatry/psychology and the State) often seems to exacerbate self-harm, what can we do? This final section looks at a range of more practical strategies that young people, workers and their supporters can adopt. Whilst these strategies do not necessarily offer 'solutions', they at least provide some useful methods to attempt to re-address the balance in young people's favour.

In Chapter 9, Sam Warner and Doug Feery describe various aspects of the law that may impact on people who self-harm and those who work with them. They pose the question *Self-Injury and the Law: What choices do we really have?* This chapter draws our attention to the legal context underpinning our ability to work in more permissive ways with young people. It identifies laws that prevent people from self-harming in certain (often secure) settings, and identifies aspects of law that can be used to secure people's rights and choices. It also highlights the benefits of using advocates and expert witnesses to further enable rights and choices. In Chapter 10, Carolyn McQueen explores how restrictive laws and contexts around self-harm can be worked with and challenged. She takes as her example self-harm in young offenders institutions and offers a number of useful strategies for workers in these contexts to navigate this environment by *Weaving different practices: Working with children and young people who self-harm in prison*.

In Chapter 11, *Harm Minimisation: Limiting the damage of self-injury*, Louise Pembroke powerfully describes how it is not just people in prisons and institutions who can have their choices restricted. She argues that the problem is not just about interventions which focus on stopping people from harming themselves, but also about people having insufficient knowledge and information about self-injury, anatomy and self-care. Louise makes a convincing case for how young people can benefit from a user-led 'harm minimisation' approach to limit the damage of (even extreme forms of) self-injury. Finally, if we are going to support people to make informed choices, we need other practical measures to enable this, such as forward planning tools like 'advanced directives'. In the final chapter, Chapter 12, Helen Spandler and Pauline Heslop explore how the new funding mechanism of 'direct payments' could be used to enable people to take more control of the support they receive. In *Exercising Choice and Control: Independent living, direct payments and self-harm*, Helen and Pauline give examples of how some survivors are using mechanisms like this to develop innovative and more 'person-centred' ways of responding to self-harm.

CONCLUSIONS: A POLITICS OF SELF-HARM

As argued, improved service responses and increased awareness about self-harm has arisen in large part due to the action of survivors and their allies, principally inspired by *political* initiatives such as the feminist and psychiatric survivors' movement (Cresswell, 2005; Pembroke, 2006). If we recognise this, it seems clear that a progressive politics of self-harm remains necessary. We believe that bringing a 'politics of self-harm' into practice discussions influences the degree to which we are able to work alongside and accept people who self-harm. This progressive politics is based on three related elements.

First, it is connected to a broader agenda of challenging existing ways of evaluating and developing mental health services. This book, therefore, forms part of a new era of 'evidence-based practice'. It subverts existing hierarchies of evidence and places the views of survivors and progressive practitioners at its heart, and it also moves the focus from technique and method, to principle and value base. We hope that both these strategies might help us develop more responsive and individually tailored services that survivors value and find useful, rather than harmful.

Second, if we are going to work in progressive ways, we need a political approach that understands the impact of wider social structures. All the chapters in this book implicitly or explicitly politicise self-harm by arguing that it is crucial to reintroduce issues of power, abuse and oppression into discussions of self-harm. This is part of our principled approach to understanding self-harm. As such, all the contributions take into account the impact of the wider context in which self-harm is initiated and sustained (and often escalates) through psychiatric interventions and categorisation, social policy and oppressive social relations.

Finally, although accepting self-harm is an important step forward, ultimately a politics of self-harm needs to move beyond 'self-help' and 'damage limitation' (essential though they both are). The danger of completely accepting self-harm is that the damaging social conditions that young people experience are also accepted and unchallenged. People who self-harm may then be cajoled or coerced into learning new strategies to 'cope better' with adverse life events. Although complex 'problems in living' (Szasz, 1961) may be inevitable as young people negotiate their place in the world, the oppression and abuse many young people experience is not acceptable. Whilst it is important to recognise and respect the coping mechanisms young people have developed, it is equally vital to combat the social conditions which make self-harm seem necessary. It is these conditions which constrain people's choices such that self-harm becomes a viable option. If we challenge these conditions, then it opens up other options, both for young people themselves, and for those who seek to work alongside them.

REFERENCES

Arnold, L (1995) *Women and Self-Injury: A survey of 76 women.* Bristol: Bristol Crisis Service for Women.

Arnold, L & Magill, A (1997) What's the Harm? A book for young people who self-harm. Bristol: The Basement Project.

Asylum (1989) Survivors' News. *Asylum: The magazine for democratic psychiatry, 4* (1), 16.

Babiker, G & Arnold, L (1998) *The Language of Injury: Comprehending self-mutilation.* Leicester: BPS Books.

Burton, M & Chapman, MJ (2004) Problems of evidence-based practice in community-based services. *Journal of Intellectual Disabilities, 8* (1), 56–70.

Cooper, B (2003) Evidence-based mental health policy: A critical appraisal. *British Journal of Psychiatry, 183*, 105–13.

Cresswell, M (2005) Psychiatric survivors and testimonies of self-harm. *Social Science and Medicine 61*, 1668–77.

Department of Health (2001) *Safety First: Five-year report of the National Confidential Inquiry into Suicide and Homicide by People with Mental Illness.* London: Department of Health.

Department of Health (2002) *National Suicide Prevention Strategy for England.* London: Department of Health.

Department of Health (2003) *Mainstreaming Gender and Women's Mental Health.* London: Department of Health.

Derouin, A & Bravender, T (2004) Living on the edge: The current phenomenon of self-mutilation in adolescents. *The American Journal of Maternal & Child Nursing, 29* (1), 2– 8.

Ferguson, H (2003) Outline of a critical best practice perspective on social work and social care. *British Journal of Social Work, 33* (8), 1005–24.

Fox, C & Hawton, K (2004) *Deliberate Self-Harm in Adolescence.* London: Jessica Kingsley Publishers.

Hawton, K & van Heeringen, K (eds) (2000) *The International Handbook of Suicide and Attempted Suicide.* Chichester: John Wiley & Sons.

Humphries, B (2003) What else counts as evidence in evidence-based social work? *Social Work Education, 22* (1), 81–91.

Lefevre, SJ (1996) *Killing Me Softly: Self-harm, survival not suicide.* Gwynedd: Handsell Publications.

MHF (2006) *Truth Hurts—Report of the National Inquiry into Self-Harm among Young People.* London: Mental Health Foundation.

NICE (2004) Self-harm: The short-term physical and psychological management and secondary prevention of intentional self-harm in primary and secondary care. *Clinical Guideline 16.* London: NICE (National Institute for Clinical Excellence).

Norton, K & Dolan, B (1996) Acting out and the institutional response. In B Dolan (ed) *Perspectives on Henderson Hospital* (pp. 74–92). Sutton, Surrey: The Henderson Hospital.

Parker, I (2007) *Revolution in Psychology: Alienation to emancipation*. London: Pluto Press.

Pembroke, L (1994) *Self-harm: Perspectives from personal experience*. London: Survivors Speak Out.

Pembroke, L (2006) We need a user-led and informed debate about how best to respond to people who self-harm. *Mental Health Today*, July/Aug 2006, 16–18.

Pope, C (2003) Resisting evidence: The study of evidence-based medicine as a contemporary movement. *Health: An Interdisciplinary Journal for the Study of Health, Illness and Medicine*, 7 (3), 267–82.

SDC & RUHBC (2005) *Written on the Body: A review of literature on self-cutting*. Paper prepared for the National Inquiry into Self-Harm among Young People, June 2005. Scottish Development Centre for Mental Health & Research Unit in Health, Behaviour and Change, University of Edinburgh.

Smith, A & Clarke, J (2003) *Self-Harm Self-Help/Support Groups*. London: Mental Health Foundation.

Smith, A & Pembroke, L (2005) Diatribe. *Mental Health Today*, June, 35.

Spandler, H (1996) *Who's Hurting Who? Young people, self-harm and suicide*. Manchester: 42nd Street.

Szasz, TS (1961) *The Myth of Mental Illness: Foundations of a theory of personal conduct*. New York: Hoeber-Harper.

Warner, S (2000) *Understanding Child Sexual Abuse: Making the tactics visible*. Gloucester: Handsell.

Warner, S (2004) Women at the margins. *Asylum: The magazine for democratic psychiatry*, 14, 3.

Webb, SA (2001) Considerations on the validity of evidence-based practice in social work. *British Journal of Social Work*, 31, 57–79.

PART ONE:
WORKING ALONGSIDE YOUNG PEOPLE

Chapter 1

A DIALOGUE OF HOPE AND SURVIVAL

Clare Shaw and Terri Shaw

Clare

It was a Sunday morning and mum was at Mass. I was fifteen. I pried the blade out of a safety razor, and repeatedly cut the palm of my hand. I still remember what it looked like. I still remember the hot, red feeling of the blood pooling in my hand. I have no memories of any other feelings, even pain.

I prepared my cover story thoroughly. I propped the sharp bread knife in the sink so that I could demonstrate to my mum how I had accidentally cut myself. This is the story I repeated in A&E.

It wasn't the first time I'd cut myself. I remember being ten and making little cuts in my lips with nail clippers. I took small overdoses, stealing my father's painkillers. I had no idea of what I was doing and why I was doing it—I just knew that it was wrong and must be kept secret.

It was the same as I got older. I swallowed 20 paracetamol and a bottle of cough mixture. I was sick all night and day but told no one what I'd done. I was fifteen. I had a crush on my friend. I started to keep myself awake at nights, watching television in my bedroom, writing poetry. One night I cut my wrists. Unhappy people—really unhappy people—cut their wrists. That's all I knew. I tried to keep it hidden, but at the same time, I wanted someone to see.

I started to starve myself. More than anything, I wanted to be thin. So thin that people would stand and stare. I got ill. I was told off for missing classes. Teachers were worried that this high-achieving pupil was going to mess up. I was so hungry! I discovered how to make myself vomit, like all my sisters had. Now I could eat all I wanted and still get thinner.

It became an obsession. It got better, it got worse; it got a whole lot worse. I made good friends at sixth form. I came out as a dyke—not easy in a Catholic school in Burnley. I got a girlfriend. I studied hard. I starved, binged, vomited, every day. It was a way of life. I hardly noticed it anymore.

My girlfriend didn't know about the eating. But she knew that sometimes I cut myself. Sometimes I would bang my head against the wall. I scared her. Sometimes she would lock me in the room. She said that I needed to see a psychiatrist. I thought this was a stupid idea!

We split up. I started seeing someone else. For the first time in my life, I felt more unhappy than I could cope with. I was twenty years old. I thought about death all the time. I told my friend, who told me to speak to a doctor, who referred me to the university psychiatrist.

He was a small man. He diagnosed 'Third-Year Nerves' and gave me Prozac. It wasn't long until my twenty-first birthday. It went badly. Shortly after, I took an overdose of Prozac. I was admitted to a medical ward, and then to the psychiatric ward.

This was my entry into the psychiatric system.

Terri

I was totally stunned when I heard the news that my younger sister Clare had been admitted to hospital having taken an overdose. Nothing like that had ever happened in our family and I couldn't believe that things had got so bad for Clare without me having the slightest clue. However, I gained some consolation from the fact that Clare was still alive and at least she was now in hospital.

Knowing that Clare was in hospital, I hoped that she would now be given whatever help she needed and I also gained a measure of comfort by thinking that she was being cared for in a safe environment. It is hard to define what I meant by 'safe'—the dictionary defines it as 'free from harm or risk, no longer in danger' and I think this fits in with my own understanding of the word. Following on from this understanding, I presumed that the environment would be one in which Clare would be kept free from harm or risk, whether from other people or from herself. I don't believe that this expectation was unreasonable: indeed, it is a basic principle described by Florence Nightingale when she said that a hospital shall do the patient no harm.

I travelled to Liverpool the next day to visit Clare, still too shocked to give any real consideration as to what to expect. Nothing however could have prepared me for my initial reaction on entering the acute psychiatric ward that she had been admitted to. I couldn't even begin to describe that feeling of overwhelming horror as I walked through those doors: the noise, the dirt, the chaos, the locks and bolts on all the doors and windows. I remember thinking that it was just like the film One Flew Over the Cuckoo's Nest. *I recently asked my daughter Carla if she remembered the ward that Auntie Clare was first admitted to. Carla, who would only have been about 5 at the time, turned to me and said, 'Oh mum, it was like a prison; it was like the worst place ever'.*

So, it wasn't the 'safe' environment I was hoping for, but still at least Clare was going to get some help. Or so I thought. In reality, it was difficult to see just what was being done to help Clare. I knew she was being given some pretty heavy medication because there were times when I visited Clare that she was so 'doped up' she was incapable of stringing a sentence together. Maybe that was the idea—to sedate Clare to the point that she was physically incapable of harming herself? Yet when Clare was in hospital, she not only continued harming herself, but the injuries she inflicted on those occasions were so much worse than the ones she had done when at home. I vividly remember the phone call that told us that Clare needed surgery because she had cut through the tendons in her arm.

No one took the time to talk to us, or to try and explain anything. That was the worst thing about the experience—not knowing what was happening, not knowing what was going to happen. All we knew was that Clare was suffering and we didn't know how to help her. We lived with the constant fear that Clare was trying to kill herself—not knowing or understanding anything about self-injury, we thought that that was what she was trying to do. Our mother remembers begging the consultant to section Clare because she didn't know what else to do and she just wanted to try and keep Clare safe.

And yes, I suppose in theory, stripping Clare of her personal possessions (and dignity), not allowing her access to anything that might provide some form of distraction or relief, not allowing her the privacy to talk to family or friends or to go for a walk or even the canteen was one way of attempting to prevent her from harming herself. But at what cost? In any case, it didn't work. She was still self-injuring, more frequently and more severely than ever. It was at this point that I began to wonder just what Clare was doing in hospital, or rather just what exactly was the hospital doing for her—except making things worse?

INPATIENT SERVICES

Dissatisfaction with the psychiatric system is not new, nor is it uncommon. For as long as psychiatry has existed, patients and their allies have expressed profound concerns about almost every aspect of the system (see, for example, Porter, 1990; Johnstone, 2000). In recent years, these concerns have been the focus of social movements such as the anti-psychiatry movement, the women's health movement, and of course, the service user/survivor movement.

The opinions and experiences of the psychiatric patient have, historically, been marginalised and disregarded within psychiatric research and theory (Rogers et al., 1993). Where they *have* been recorded, they often provide us with stark insight into the experience of the wards:

> I was fastened down in a bed; a meagre diet was ordered for me; this and medicine forced down my throat or in the contrary direction; my will, my wishes, my repugnances, my habits, my delicacy, my inclinations, my necessities, were not consulted. (Perceval, 1838/40: 179)

> As you go through those ward doors, 'Abandon hope all ye who enter here'. (Rita, in Patiniotis, 2005: 11)

This is compounded for patients who, because of their age, gender, sexuality, abilities or ethnic identity, are even more likely to have their needs for support disregarded or marginalised within services (see, for example, Bloefeld, 2003; Department of Health, 1999; Ussher, 1992; Wright & Anthony, 2002). Young people who use mental health services face additional problems and pressures, including an increased difficulty in accessing services which are appropriate to their age and needs, and which are in their home area. Given this, it isn't surprising that research such as Rogers, Pilgrim and Lacey's national survey (1993) and Patiniotis' regional survey of inpatients (2005) indicate that the experience of inpatients is often negative:

> I hated hospital life—it made me crack up even more. People didn't seem to care. (respondent in Rogers et al., 1993: 63)

Levels of dissatisfaction with services amongst people who self-injure are particularly high. In the Bristol Crisis Service national survey of women who self-injure, only 4 per cent of women expressed satisfaction with their experience of inpatient services (Arnold, 1995). Service responses that were reported as 'unhelpful' included: 'condemnatory, dismissive and punitive attitudes'; 'ignorance and misunderstanding'; 'failure to listen to or address underlying issues'; 'inappropriate or inadequate treatment'; and 'being subject to excessive or abusive power or control'. Unsurprisingly, young people who self-injure often report negative experiences of inpatient services: 'They made me feel that I was a waste of time and space' (respondent in Spandler, 1996: 72). The consequences of these negative experiences are predictable: already high levels of distress are increased; already shattered levels of self-esteem are further eroded and the need to self-injure is increased.

Clare

We slept in dormitories of six with curtains around the bed. I was twenty-two. It had been a very bad day. I found a razor in the washing area and took it to my cubicle. I had to use it as much as I could, as quickly as I could, before I was found and stopped. I hid in the space between my bed and the cupboards, behind the curtain.

It was dark in there. I started by cutting my legs. It wasn't enough. I cut my wrists and forearms, again and again, without looking at what I was doing. The blood came out like never before. I got frightened and shouted for help. I needed over 130 stitches, and surgery to my left wrist.

During my months on different inpatient units, I cut myself with razors. I re-opened sutures, I inserted objects and rubbed dirt into open wounds, I injured myself with broken glass and crockery, I gouged myself with a fork and I cut myself with a ripped-up can. I punched myself repeatedly, I banged my head on the wall, I overdosed,

I hung myself from the back of the bathroom door until I lost consciousness, and daily, I binged and vomited and starved. These were all units that did not allow self-harm.

All my self-harm had to take place in private, inflicted as quickly and as severely as possible, using whatever means were to hand. Despite being on 'close observation' it was worse than ever. This continued throughout the six years I spent in and out of inpatient wards.

Terri

Throughout Clare's years of self-injury I lived with the belief that she was suicidal. This seemed to be the only possible explanation for why she was cutting herself and taking overdoses. It came as a revelation when I discovered that, on the basis of what people who self-injure say about their own experiences, self-injury actually serves as a coping mechanism. More often than not, self-injury helps to avert suicidal feelings—it is a way to stay alive. I wish that somebody had explained this to me at the time or referred me to any of the resources that exist for carers (e.g. Arnold, 1997).

However, this realisation still did not explain why Clare's self-injury had worsened so dramatically whilst she was in the psychiatric environment. Through conversations with Clare, and through hearing accounts from other people who spent time in hospital, I started to question the approach to self-injury that had been taken by the hospitals that Clare was detained in. I became aware that there were other possible ways of working, being put into practice across the UK by people who self-injure and the people that work with them—underlaid by an approach that might be loosely described as 'harm minimisation' or 'safer self-harm'. I decided to focus specifically on harm minimisation for my postgraduate research study, which we refer to in the next section.

STOPPING SELF-INJURY

The self-harming behaviour is never addressed other than 'you don't do it'. (Shaw, 2004: 36)

The approach taken by the hospitals where Clare was treated reflects current dominant practice around self-injury, which is aimed at stopping people from self-injuring whilst they are in hospital. This reflects what the Mental Health Act Code of Practice (Department of Health, 1999) says about 'patients at risk of self-injury'—that 'patients must be protected from harming themselves when the drive to self-injure is the result of a mental disorder for which they are receiving care and treatment' (Department of Health, 1999: 18.30). Given that the general assumption is that self-injury is indicative of the presence of a mental disorder—often 'Borderline Personality Disorder'—it follows that most services understand themselves as being under a professional, legal and ethical obligation to stop their patients from self-harming. Attempts are made to enforce 'no self-harm policies' by interventions to keep people away from items that could be used for self-injury. Rooms are stripped and patients are deprived of personal belongings that are viewed as potential harming objects, patients are controlled and restrained (Hogg, 2001), and may be placed in seclusion (Liebling et al., 1997).

However, as this book suggests, there is a growing body of opinion that this emphasis on stopping self-injury simply does not work, and is both unrealistic and potentially more harmful (e.g. Arnold, 1995; Pembroke, 1996; Spandler, 1996; Harris, 2000; Hogg, 2001). In practice, it appears to be impossible to prevent someone from self-injuring regardless of what restrictions are put in place. Furthermore, as the self-injury takes place in a very 'out of control' manner because of the methods used and because of the need for secrecy and urgency, it follows then that the injuries that result are potentially more damaging: 'I did much, much more damage than I ever did at home' (Shaw, 2004: 27).

WHO'S HURTING WHO?

It also seems that the hospital environment substantially increases the need to self-injure. Research establishes again and again that self-injury often functions as a mechanism for coping with painful feelings and situations (Arnold, 1995; Spandler, 1996), and that services are often experienced as invalidating, punitive and hostile (Arnold, 1995; Pembroke, 1996; Rogers et al., 1993; Spandler, 1996). It follows then that the situation that people may be trying to cope with through self-injury is the service response itself; and the feelings that people are trying to cope with are those provoked by that response: 'totally disregarded and made to feel even worse' (Shaw, 2004: 37).

Despite the increased distress experienced as a result of the psychiatric environment, 'no self-harm' policies often prevent the patient from accessing other forms of coping strategies. Patients can be prevented from leaving the ward, or from accessing objects such as pens to write with. Opportunities for constructive dialogue are restricted as staff and patients engage in a 'cat and mouse game' of trying to enforce and circumvent 'no self-harm' policies; and feelings of powerlessness are confirmed and worsened as more and more restrictions are enforced against the patient (Shaw, 2004; Shaw & Hogg, 2004). This leads to the paradoxical situation whereby the 'no self-harm' approach can actually increase the frequency and severity of self-injury, and may even contribute towards suicidal thoughts and feelings (Bourne, 2001). A potential way of minimising this harm is to enable patients to self-injure in a safer, more controlled way—safer self-harm.

RESEARCHING SAFER SELF-HARM

Views vary about how to achieve safer self-harm. It could be partially achieved simply through the knowledge that it is acceptable to self-injure, which would reduce the pressure, blame, secrecy and urgency around the act of self-injury (Pembroke, 1996). Some people understand it as an issue around information such as knowing where to cut to achieve maximum psychological benefit with minimal physical damage (National Self Harm Network, 1997). For other people it is more proactive and may involve making clean blades and dressings available (e.g. Hogg, 2001; Clarke, 1998; Hewitt, 2004). But what unites all these different approaches is the belief that stopping people from self-injuring at all costs is counterproductive and can actually increase the harm.

With this in mind, one of us (Terri) undertook a small-scale study of student nurses' and ex-patients' perspectives on safer self-injury within a local psychiatric inpatient setting (Shaw, 2004). Consultation took place with a focus group of young women who self-injured and had experience of using services; as well as a focus group of student nurses who had all worked with people who self-injure. The following quotes are taken from this study. The women who self-injured discussed the functions that their self-injury had served for them, and how it had enabled them to survive overwhelming feelings of distress. They did not emphasise proactive approaches such as the issuing of clean blades; rather, they advocated harm-minimisation strategies that focused on the provision of information and resources on self-care and managing the aftercare of the wounds. They discussed strategies such as learning first aid so that they could treat the wound, and knowing how to recognise the signs of infection so that they could take antibiotics.

Like Clare, the women had previously formed their own version of 'safer self-injury' through 'trial and error'—by inflicting unintended damage on themselves and thus learning how not to cut in order to limit the damage. Their view was that information on safer self-injury would be used constructively to lessen the damage rather than to increase it. The women had all experienced inpatient services where practice was based on the assumption that they must be prevented from self-harming. None of the women found this helpful. All continued to self-harm, often more frequently and severely. They experienced the emphasis on stopping their self-injury as negative because it prevented honest and meaningful dialogue between patients and staff—'don't tell them what you are feeling—you'd never get out' (Shaw, 2004: 28); it meant that the focus of treatment was on self-harm prevention rather than exploring the distress and the deeper issues behind the act; and that it prevented access to other valuable coping strategies: 'when

I wanted to self-harm I'd distract myself, go out for walks—you can't do that in hospital' (Shaw, 2004: 30).

Likewise, the staff group were critical of the consequences of an emphasis on stopping self-harm as this shifted the focus of treatment from care to custody: 'we become policeman not nurses' (Shaw, 2004: 38). The nurses also felt that risk was increased because of the restrictions as the methods used by patients to self-harm would be far more dangerous and this risk was further increased because of the need for secrecy—'it's all behind closed doors and locked rooms' (ibid: 38). They felt that Risk Assessment procedures ought to take into account the fact that the patient had the knowledge of how to self-harm without causing any permanent damage 'he's very aware of what he uses and knows how to care for it and everything' (ibid: 37).

This suggests the need for a different interpretation of risk: namely, people who self-injure may be well qualified to manage the risk inherent in their self-injury; and that the risk we should be addressing is the equal or greater risk that over-controlling and restrictive services can inflict upon distressed people—who's hurting who? It also suggests that safer self-injury may be a valid method of working with people who self-injure, as a way of reducing risk and increasing safety.

The emphasis on stopping self-injury at all costs undoubtedly contributes to the negative experience that people who self-injure often have within inpatient environments. As we have described, this emphasis removes a valuable and functional coping mechanism from people at a point when they are most likely to need it. It also often leads to the removal of other means of coping with or reducing distress. It can add to the need to self-injure by removing control, privacy and dignity from the distressed person; and it can reduce an already shattered sense of self-esteem by confirming to the person that what they are doing is wrong. It obstructs meaningful relationships with staff who are required to act as 'policemen', and from whom the need to self-injure or acts of actual self-harm must be kept secret.

For people who self-injure, this can mean that inpatient treatment is experienced as punitive or controlling, rather than as caring or supportive. This places great pressure on staff, who can feel a sense of failure and responsibility as they are not able to prevent people from hurting themselves, and a sense of frustration at not being able to provide the meaningful support to people in distress. Indeed, anecdotal evidence indicates that many staff are already carrying out practices that fall within the spectrum of safer self-harm/ harm minimisation practice, albeit informally and without the legal and practical support of management, guidelines or NHS Trust policy. All of this indicates that the practice of safer self-injury within inpatient settings would be a positive way forward in the effort to improve services for people who self-injure; and that this should be recognised at a trust and policy level. However, the research also highlights the complex questions that must be engaged with as part of such a shift.

COMPLEXITIES

As we have described, harm minimisation practice can include a range of different approaches, each of which will have different legal, practical and ethical implications (Hewitt, 2004; Shaw, 2004). For example, the women who self-injure expressed reservations about more pro-active approaches such as having access to clean blades in a ward environment. They agreed that having unlimited access to blades on psychiatric wards as they exist now, could potentially increase risk and that 'safer self-injury' would demand some profound changes in ward culture. This was based on their understanding of self-harm as a coping mechanism and how they perceived the psychiatric environment to increase the need to self-injure:

> 'I think the worst case scenario would be to be locked up in such a horrible place as the psychiatric ward and given access to blades 'cos, bloody hell, I would be using them way more 'cos it's such a horrible environment' (Shaw, 2004: 30)

Consequently, rather than limiting their focus to the practical and legal specifics addressed (see Hewitt, 2004), the issue of self-harm prompted both groups to grapple with the wider question of: 'How do you make better a system that's fundamentally flawed?' (Shaw, 2004: 58). This question suggests that 'safer self-harm' policies may constitute just the starting point in the process of changing services so that they respond more helpfully to people who self-injure.

CREATING BETTER SERVICES

Self-injury is a complex and individual experience. Yet evidence which is based upon the experiences of people who self-injure consistently reflects similar themes in what service responses are experienced as helpful or unhelpful. These can be loosely grouped as: dismissive, hostile, and punitive responses; being subject to excessive power and control; not being listened to; not having access to counselling or therapy; being subject to stigmatising labels (Arnold, 1995; Spandler, 1996; Walker, 2004). People who self-injure also name environmental issues—such as services being characterised by dirt, danger, noise and chaos; as well as the age and gender inappropriate services offered to young women such as mixed-sex inpatient wards, and being admitted to an adult inpatient ward at the age of seventeen (Shaw, 2004).

Clare

A day begins at seven when I'm woken by the sound of staff and the other patients in my dormitory. I sleep by the door with my bed curtain open so that staff can carry out their fifteen-minute observations. Sometimes we can persuade one of the staff to let us have a cup of tea before breakfast arrives. The corridors and bathrooms grow busy with men and women in their pyjamas. The day starts. Morning telly and cigarettes. Mid-morning tea break. I'm careful which men are around, what level of trouble I should expect.

Lunchtime. We call the food 'brown stuff'. Mandy stubs her cigarette out on her plate and goes back to bed. Afternoon telly and cigarettes. Mid-afternoon tea and biscuits. A visitor—we sit together in the canteen which smells of brown stuff. Chips for tea. Evening draws in. Telly. Cigarettes. I find it hard to read. I clean the floor under my bed. Two hundred sit-ups. I'm allowed into the locked lobby of the hospital to buy snacks from the machine: chocolate, crisps, coke. I take it back to my cubicle; eat it quietly, throw it back up. Sometimes I rip the can up and use it to cut myself. Every fifteen minutes, a face looks through the door, ticks a box. I'm still alive.

Listening to the voices of people who self-injure—and the voices of the friends, partners, family and staff who care for them—reminds us of the urgent need for change in the way that inpatient (and other) services respond to self-injury. People who self-injure are clear about what they want and need from services—acceptance, respect, caring, support (Arnold, 1995). These are not unreasonable expectations. Yet creating services which are characterised by these qualities will demand some profound shifts in current service culture. A willingness to acknowledge the need for harm minimisation practice must form part of those changes.

CODA: ALTOGETHER NOW

Terri

Each day stretched into weeks and each week stretched into months of slowly beginning to hope that there might be a future for Clare after all. A future of normal family things like going out for lunch or phone calls when you have each other in hysterics over something that has happened that day. Evenings spent in the pub together, getting drunk, putting the world to rights. There was a time when I never thought this would happen, a time when I never dared hope that Clare would survive.

It is said that 'hindsight is a wonderful thing', but this is only true if lessons can be learned from past experiences. It is difficult, with the knowledge I have gained over the years, not to look back at the time Clare spent in hospital without feeling a deep sense of bitterness and betrayal. That the system I had placed so much hope and faith in failed Clare in just about every sense of the word. My only hope is that people will start listening, and take action to ensure that some other family isn't telling the same story years down the line.

Words cannot convey my overwhelming pride and respect for Clare's strength, courage and desire to live. And for surviving, not only the traumas that led to her self-injury, but for coming out the other end of a system that almost succeeded in destroying her.

Clare

With help and with love, I found my own way back. I went on to experience good, meaningful support from professionals—my therapist; my housing support worker; from caring individuals working creatively within the limits imposed on them within inpatient settings; and from other people who self-injure. It was a long, rough road. For much of the way, I still needed to injure myself to survive enduring feelings of distress. But I never again injured myself as severely as I did when I was in hospital. I'm a walker, a rock climber and a writer; I play the violin and the guitar, so I don't want to lose my mobility, the use of my hands. Through my own experiences, and through the work of organisations like the National Self Harm Network, I learnt how to minimise the harm that I inflicted on myself.

Five years have passed since my last admission to an inpatient ward. My life has changed dramatically and though, of course, I still have bad days, I no longer injure myself in the ways that I used to. An important element of my recovery has been my involvement in self-harm activism: working with other people who self-harm and our allies to increase understanding and awareness of self-harm; and to challenge the unhelpful responses that characterised much of my experience of inpatient services. I'm now working in a training partnership with Terri to provide training to staff who work with people who self-injure, both of us speaking from the immense depth of knowledge and commitment which arises from our experiences of self-harm; and experiencing the fulfillment that comes from making a positive difference.

As I write this, I'm sitting at my window on a winter's day. My cat is asleep in the doorway. I'm looking at my arms, which are written all over with the evidence of all my battles. Which are scarred and muscled and tanned. And very, very strong. The sky is clear and beautifully blue.

REFERENCES

Arnold, L (1995) *Women and Self-Injury: A survey of 76 women.* Bristol: Bristol Crisis Service for Women.

Arnold, L (1997) *Women and Self-injury—For friends and family.* Bristol: Bristol Crisis Service for Women.

Blofeld, J (2003) *Independent Inquiry into the death of David Bennett.* Published by Norfolk, Suffolk and Cambridgeshire Strategic Health Authority, December 2003.

Bourne, SL (2001) *Women and self-injury; figuring out the hidden agenda. A legal and ethical challenge to health care professionals.* Unpublished thesis, Manchester University, Faculty of Education.

Breggin, P (1993) *Toxic Psychiatry.* London: Mind.

Department of Health (1999) *Facing the Facts: Services for people with learning difficulties.* UK: The Stationery Office.

Department of Health (1999) *Code of Practice to the Mental Health Act.* UK: The Stationery Office.

Clarke, L (1998) Self-mutilation, culture, contexts and nursing responses. *Journal of Clinical Nursing, 7* (2), 129–37.

Duffy, D & Ryan, T (2004) (eds) *New Approaches to Preventing Suicide: A manual for practitioners.* London: Jessica Kingsley.

Harris, J (2000) Self-harm: Cutting the bad out of me. *Qualitative Health Research, 10* (2), 164–73.

Hewitt, D (2004) Assisting self-harm—Some legal considerations. In D Duffy & T Ryan (eds) *New Approaches to Preventing Suicide: A manual for practitioners* (pp. 148–66). London: Jessica Kingsley.

Hogg, C (2001) Should nurses always intervene when patients self-harm? *Nursing Times, 97,* 49.

Johnstone, J (2000) *Users and Abusers of Psychiatry* (second edn). London: Routledge.

Liebling, H, Chipchase, H & Velangi, R (1997) Why do women harm themselves?—Surviving special hospitals. *Feminism and Psychology, 7* (3), 427–37.

National Self Harm Network (1997) *Cutting the Risk: Self-harm, self-care and risk reduction.* London: National Self Harm Network.

Patiniotis, J (2005) *Who's Listening? Gender sensitive mental health provision: Key issues from the perspectives of service users.* Merseyside: PPI Forum.

Pembroke, L (ed) (1996) *Self-harm: Perspectives from personal experience.* London: Survivors Speak Out.

Perceval, J (1838/40) *A Narrative of the Treatment Received/Experienced by a Gentleman During a State of Mental Derangement.* London: Effingham Wilson.

Porter, R (1990) *Mind Forg'd Manacles: A history of madness in England from the Restoration to the Regency.* Harmondsworth: Penguin.

Rogers, A, Pilgrim, D & Lacey, R (1993) *Experiencing Psychiatry—User's views of services.* London: MacMillan.

Shaw, C & Hogg, C (2004) Shouting at the Spaceman—A conversation about self-harm. In D Duffy & T Ryan (eds) *New Approaches to Preventing Suicide: A manual for practitioners* (pp. 167–77). London: Jessica Kingsley.

Shaw, T (2004) *Different Voices: A small scale study of student nurses and ex-patients. Perspectives on safer self-injury within a British psychiatric inpatient setting.* Unpublished MA Dissertation, UCLAN.

Spandler, H (1996) *Who's Hurting Who? Young people, self-harm and suicide.* Manchester: 42nd Street.

Ussher, J (1992) *Women's Madness: Misogyny or mental illness?* London: Harvester Wheatshead.

Walker, T (2004) Why Cut Up? *Asylum 14,* (3), 20–2.

Wright, R & Anthony, P (2002) Lesbians and mental health: are we helping or hindering? *Mental Health Care, 5* (8), 12–15.

Chapter 2

EDGES AND LEDGES:
YOUNG PEOPLE AND INFORMAL SUPPORT
AT 42ND STREET

EAMONN KIRK

I have spent nights with matches and knives
Leaning over ledges, only two flights up
Cutting my heart, burning my soul, nothing left to hold
Nothing left but blood and fire ...

I am intense, I am in need, I am in pain ...

(Blood and Fire, The Indigo Girls, 1989)

INTRODUCTION

I have something in common with lawyers, estate agents and traffic wardens
(with apologies to all three professions). In my social life, when asked what
my job is, I hesitate before I reply, anticipating a mixed reaction once I've
told people. The job title 'Suicide and Self-harm Worker' can be a conversation
stopper. Then things can get slightly hysterical when it becomes clear I work
with young people, followed by bewilderment that I make a positive, definite
choice to do this type of work, and that I enjoy it.

This is a great indicator of where self-harm and suicide can often be
located with respect to a person's comfort zone: that is, outside of it, or just
on the edges. I'm not passing judgement as it's taken me a while, as well as
some profound experiences and reflections, to place suicide and self-harm
within my own comfort zone. However, what all this can show is that often
the response to self-harm and suicidal feelings is a very personal and emotional
one. And indeed, as the quote at the beginning of this article suggests, self-
harm and suicidal feelings are emotional subjects, especially for the person
directly struggling with these, and also for family, friends, and workers.

The following are some reflections on being in post for three years as a
Suicide and Self-harm Worker, providing informal support to young people
at 42nd Street. The chapter looks at what seems to work in supporting young

people who self-harm and/or have suicidal feelings. It identifies particular patterns in the work as well as examining the support needs of workers. I've tried to touch on key themes throughout the article, such as focusing on young people, my relationships with them, as well as looking at choices and risks.

I'm sharing these reflections in the hope that they may take away some of the mythology and mystique often associated with this work, and perhaps give some confidence to workers who might be struggling, especially people who aren't trained therapists or counsellors. In addition, I'm writing with the aim of encouraging people, especially young people, who want support with issues of suicide and self-harm, to seek such help. Rather than being academic or theoretical, the style of this chapter reflects the informal approach I take in my work. I hope it shows how, at 42nd Street, we try to work with young people who are often at the edge of something, be it the edge of a crisis or a breakthrough, the edge of a community, the edge of a knife or a window ledge two flights up.

HOW DID I GET HERE?

I've had varied experiences that led me to 42nd Street. While studying for my first degree, I was a cleaner on psychiatric wards, including those where people had been sectioned under the Mental Health Act (1983). The impact of seeing people in deep crises, with acute mental health issues, did two things. One was to awaken my passion for mental health work, and the other was to force me to look deeply at myself and my own coping mechanisms.

After a stint in science publishing, working in a Citizens Advice Bureau, and some therapy of my own, I became a residential support worker for people with mental health needs. I then went on to complete a Diploma and Masters in Psychiatric Social Work, including a placement in an adult mental health day centre and a stint in Child and Adolescent Mental Health Services. Throughout these experiences, along with personal ones, working around self-harm and suicide increasingly became a dominant theme. In particular, some of the accounts from people I worked with had a lasting impact on me, and helped me to decide to pursue further experience in these areas.

I specifically wanted to work at 42nd Street in order to combine a desire to work with young people around mental health, especially suicide and self-harm, and to work in a place with similar values to my own. I'd heard it was a place where there were clear attempts to empower young people. Exploring these values is a whole separate piece of writing, but some insight into such values can be found in McDermott (1986), Davies (2000) and Spandler (1996).

WHAT WORKS FOR YOUNG PEOPLE WHO SELF-HARM?

For me, there is no mystery here. Much of the following is informed by listening to young people's voices, experiences, and hearing what they want from mental health (and other) workers. Plenty has been written in the past about service users' experiences of poor service provision (see Babiker & Arnold, 1997; Pembroke, 1994; Spandler, 1996). My sense, at least in the arenas I work in, is that things have changed for the better in many ways, but there is progress to be made.

I still meet young people who feel they have been made to wait excessively for medical attention after self-harming, or feel the way they are communicated with whilst being treated compounds the feelings that lead them to self-harm or attempt suicide. Many of these young people are astute observers, and see this treatment as based upon a moral judgement by the service provider on how they came to harm in the first place.

That said, the majority of people I work with are referred through mental health services linked to Accident & Emergency departments. Undoubtedly, a lot of the initial contact that these services have with young people, who have attempted suicide or are self-harming, affects how these young people will engage with somewhere like 42nd Street. I have heard plenty of anecdotal accounts from young people suggesting that they are treated kindly and appropriately at A&E. Arguably, a level of positive consistency between and within services will prepare young people for any therapeutic process; indeed, it may often be part of this process. To spell it out; if a young person presents at A&E with cut wrists, and is treated sensitively and non-judgementally, then surely this will encourage the young person to approach this service again, as well as others, such as 42nd Street.

Within 42nd Street, young people are offered a choice of support at the earliest possible moment with respect to whatever they bring, whether linked to self-harm, suicidal feelings, or a whole host of other areas. There is a level of consistency around working with self-harm and suicidal feelings within 42nd Street, which is embedded in its ethos: that it is OK for young people and workers to talk about these issues openly. Young people may be offered informal support, counselling, contact work/keywork, group work, drop-ins, support via our helpline, texting and e-mail. The types of support given are usually chosen by the young person, with help from a worker at 42nd Street.

There is also an attempt to offer choice regarding the gender, sexuality, ethnicity and disability of the worker wherever possible, as well as signposting to other services. Some young people would prefer to meet with a worker who reflects their own identity more closely. Some young people have less obvious motives behind their choices. For example, I have worked with some women who have been abused by men, who have chosen to work with a man. For these young women, developing trust with a male worker may be part of their healing.

Offering and respecting choices seems to communicate something important at an early stage of any relationship. Part of this is arguably about empowering young people and therefore handing over some control to them. As control is often a big issue for young people dealing with suicidal feelings or experiences of self-harm, choice in this arena seems especially sensitive.

What I feel works when beginning to engage with young people around suicidal feelings or self-harm is to actively communicate that it is OK for them to talk about these issues: I'm not going to freak out, or judge them, or tell them what to do, and the focus will be on establishing the young person's wants, needs and priorities. I have worked with a number of young people who have told me how shocked and surprised they are to realise that they're in a space where it feels OK to talk openly about issues of self-harm experiences and suicidal feelings. I've been told of a sense of relief when young people realise they will not be told off, or told to stop their self-harm, or that they 'don't really want to kill themselves'. For me, this has sometimes been put to the test (see Case Study 1).

Case Study 1

Andy was an 18-year-old young man who had been cutting his arms and chest for a few years. He came to me to find alternative ways to express his deep anger, which seemed to fuel his self-harm. We'd met five or six times, during which time he hadn't cut himself. One morning, we met and Andy was wearing a T-shirt (possibly a clue in itself). I quickly noticed his arms were covered with long, shallow, fresh scars. It seemed he wanted me to see what he had done. As part of feeding back to him, I reflected on what I saw, namely his T-shirt and scars. He told me he'd made them not long before setting off to see me. As well as checking out his self-care and whether he might need medical attention, we looked at why he might have cut himself at such a time. Andy had said in the past that he often felt quite 'up' when he knew he was coming to meet with me. It transpired that although he largely believed that I wouldn't have a go at him or criticise him for harming himself, he got up that morning and felt he needed to be sure I was true to my word. Andy didn't quite believe me up until that point, as he felt all the other professionals he'd met in his life had all wanted him to stop self-harming and, he felt, merely told him what to do.

RISK AND CONFIDENTIALITY

It is important to note that, by definition, 42nd Street's policy does put limits on what the agency can keep confidential. Like most services, 42nd Street has a confidentiality policy, which states that information may be shared within the 42nd Street team to ensure a good service for young people. Otherwise, information is not shared without permission from the young person. The exception is when a worker is concerned that there is an immediate and severe risk to a young person's life or to another person's. If this is the case, we would want to tell the young person that we are having to breach confidentiality and would support her/him through this process. This can be a difficult area to deal with, particularly when young people have been let down in the past and feel they have been the victims of unnecessary/poorly-handled breaches of confidentiality (see Case Study 2).

Case Study 2
A 17-year-old man, Jon, realised from a conversation with his mum that the family GP had been talking to her about some of Jon's difficulties. This culminated in an argument when Jon's mom told him what his GP's psychiatric diagnosis of him was. From the young man's point of view, this was without prior consent, was done without any clear need to breach confidentiality, and without an open acknowledgement that a breach had happened. Also, the fact that he had been given a diagnosis without being told made Jon even angrier. It also left Jon feeling very distrustful of service confidentiality.

As issues of control are often paramount for young people who are suicidal or self-harming, lack of care around confidentiality may be especially damaging, hence the need for transparency and honesty. In this case I supported Jon to change GPs, although he decided against any formal complaint to his former GP.

As mentioned, when involved in working with someone at 42nd Street, weighing up risk is obviously part of the initial assessment and ongoing work. Any formulation of risk is assessed through exploring a young person's self-harm and/or suicidal thoughts/feelings; the possible or actual support they receive to deal with current thoughts/feelings; an exploration of their past suicide attempts, including their feelings now about their past; and an exploration of current feelings/thoughts, including planning and protection. On the surface, this can look horribly prescriptive, but I find that usually most of this information comes out of conversation with young people, as long as I am prepared to talk openly about their past/present suicidal feelings.

Whilst 42nd Street shares similar policies to other organisations regarding disclosure of self-harm to others, differences may arise because of the way it views self-harm as a potential coping mechanism rather than suicidal in intent. This means that self-harm is not automatically seen as high risk. This is not to say that low risk is seen as unimportant. For example, some young people I work with who are not considered at a very high risk of severe harm/death can often be disregarded by statutory services. The system sometimes fails young people in high emotional pain but lower risk. An individual can be in great emotional pain and may repeatedly present at hospital, but due to a 'low risk' assessment may end up back at home, with little additional input to cope with their crisis. Therefore, at 42nd Street we try to work with young people at all stages of their distress, not just when it reaches crisis point.

The following reflections have come from work with numerous young people whose processes have all been quite different. Thus it is not intended to be prescriptive. In addition, there is obviously much overlap between these areas. However, I have noticed a pattern in how many young people define the priorities of the work to be done within sessions. A key part of this is seeing the young person as a valuable resource, who, with support, can inform her/himself.

INFORMAL SUPPORT

Informal support can be seen to encompass a spectrum of support needs and approaches. Defining informal support can prove rather difficult, especially as it is an approach that draws on many theories and schools of thought. For further discussion, see Davies (2000) and 42nd Street (2003). I see it fundamentally as a therapeutic approach for young people that allows for choice and flexibility. Some young people who pursue informal support may not be in a position to use a counselling relationship; others may be, but might *prefer* informal support because of its flexible nature.

Informal support is an attempt to combine aspects of youth work and more formal therapeutic approaches. Major 'selling points' are flexibility around the focus of the support, and also where the work happens. So, the type of informal support offered, and the venue, can change, whilst the relationship between the young person and worker is maintained. For example, informal support could be a weekly chat in a café for one young person. It could be a conversation over a game of pool or a walk in the park. For another person, it may be talking every week or fortnight in a private space about very personal issues. Informal support for one young person could be to talk about how her/his week has been. For another young person, it could mean to focus solely on practical ways of counteracting low confidence, or looking at alternatives to self-harm. For another, it may edge into discussing past and present personal and emotional issues.

Informal support can evolve; it can begin as a walk round town talking about music, football, school, and lead to deep emotional exploration in the safety of a private, confidential space. It can be as creative as any other therapeutic technique, and can involve exploring issues using art, writing and/or objects, as well as face-to-face talking. It could be seen as much more than face-to-face work, and young people I've worked with seem to value support in addition to, or instead of, face-to-face contact. This includes telephone work, mobile texting, e-mail (and maybe even the old-fashioned letter).

Many young people I've worked with chose informal support (rather than counselling) as they were in a hurry to do something about their self-harm or suicidal feelings, while wanting to understand what may lie behind these issues often came second. In other words, they wanted practical containment and reduction of the feelings behind their self-harm. These were *their* priorities compared to emotional exploration of their feelings.

A common pattern for the work I've shared with young people who are suicidal or self-harm is outlined in Figure 1. The focus of this work is on developing alternative coping strategies in the immediate and long term and, as the diagram suggests, people move between different levels of work and coping strategies at different times.

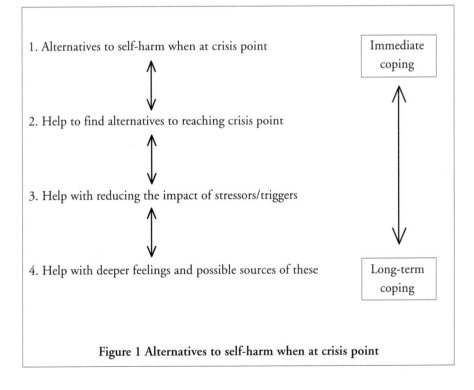

Figure 1 Alternatives to self-harm when at crisis point

Most young people already have alternatives that they use but may not have had the chance to recognise these properly. For instance, a little exploration helped one young man I worked with realise that sometimes he could, and *did,* choose to call a close friend to talk about his feelings instead of overdosing. Merely recognising this consciously seemed to allow him to choose this option more easily afterwards. It also provided a vehicle for looking at what blocked him from choosing this and other alternatives at different times.

Another common factor I have found is that many young people feel they have to have self-harmed/overdosed *before* they can go to speak to someone at A&E or elsewhere. In other words, hospitals and GPs are seen as being only for people who are physically ill or injured, or people who have already self-harmed or attempted suicide. Getting past this idea can really enable young people to access help in a preventative way.

Alternatives to self-harm can sometimes mimic physical aspects of self-harm, as well as the more emotional functions. Commonplace suggestions include using ice cubes or snapping an elastic band on the arms. Other alternatives perhaps only need to help someone achieve the more emotional reward of self-harm. I've found that after helping people identify the alternatives they already employ, it is useful to explore what others in a similar position have suggested. In fact, there are obviously hundreds of suggestions available, and I've used lists of these to help young people explore new ideas. What is interesting is that it is often an emotional response to a suggested alternative that indicates if it will work. The flip side of this is that people often have an instinct of what won't work. It helps to acknowledge that trying new things does not guarantee they will work. With young people exploring alternatives I've found it useful to reiterate that if they use something that seems to make things worse, then try something else.

HELP WITH REDUCING THE IMPACT OF EVERYDAY STRESS/TRIGGERS AND FINDING ALTERNATIVES TO REACHING CRISIS POINT

Reducing the impact of everyday stress/triggers usually involves seeing how the young person can learn to cope with the underlying feelings that seem to lead to a desire to harm themselves. These feelings commonly include anxiety, stress or anger. Practical techniques to recognise these feelings, and to reduce them, appear to work. These include techniques to deal with stress/triggers when they arise, but also there is a maintenance aspect, for example making relaxation a part of everyday life, even if some days are good days (see Case Study 3.)

Case Study 3
I was working with a 19-year-old man, Rob, and we were looking at what people do to relax. He seemed quite inhibited in terms of what he could do to help himself de-stress on a regular basis. I decided to tell him that to de-stress I danced around my living room, by myself, listening to loud music. I felt a bit self-conscious about revealing this, but we used this example as a way of looking at how de-stressing can be done in a personal and creative way, and how it can be helpful to be open-minded about what might work. At the next session, the young man (slightly sheepishly) told me that he'd given it a go and had actually found it really enjoyable and relaxing.

Sharing ideas about alternatives to self-harm, either from one's own life or other young people's, may be useful even though the alternatives might seem to be obvious, silly or familiar. Of course, ultimately it is up to the young person to decide whether they are useful or not. I've found it helpful to group these alternative coping strategies into the following categories, which take into consideration the many alternatives that have been suggested by young people themselves:

☆ Direct self-harm substitutes (these often *directly* mimic the feel/action/act of self-harm);

☆ Activities as a self-harm substitute;

☆ Increasing awareness of the 'here and now';

☆ Meditation/bodily awareness;

☆ Trying to change perspective;

☆ Delaying/distracting;

☆ Creative techniques (writing, drawing, painting, etc.);

☆ Finding/having a voice and using it.

Sometimes the things that have benefited people greatly have involved linking in with other agencies who can supply practical help that 42nd Street cannot. For instance, a young man came to me with numerous difficulties, including self-harm and suicidal feelings. We prioritised what support he wanted, and through the work we did together it emerged that money was a huge stressor. I supported him to get some benefits advice from a specialist agency, and soon he was getting the benefits he was really entitled to. This greatly helped his stress levels and helped him to cope better with his desires to cut himself and overdose. Another example is given below (see Case Study 4).

Case Study 4

A young woman I was working with, Amita, was being harassed by an ex-partner, and although he was legally meant to stay away from Amita's home, he did not. By linking up with a law agency, we established together what Amita's rights were, and how she could use these to keep her ex-partner away from her home. Just by knowing her rights, without necessarily enforcing them in any way, Amita felt much more in control of the situation, and she clearly linked this with a reduction in her desire to self-harm. She later went on to inform her ex-partner of proposed legal action if he didn't leave her alone ... this had the desired effect.

I've been involved in numerous situations where some very practical help seems to have been just as beneficial as intentionally therapeutic support. What this also highlights is the importance of partnership with other agencies, and also how useful it is to be able to signpost people to other services that may be able to help in ways that 42nd Street cannot.

Help with finding alternatives to reaching crisis point involves identifying what might make a person more likely to self-harm, and helping them to recognise their own escalation process and triggers that lead to a crisis. The key here seems to be breaking down the process of reaching crisis point, in order to increase awareness of any common events, patterns or factors. With this information, young people can start to find other options before they find themselves deep in a crisis where their likely action is to self-harm or attempt suicide.

HELP WITH UNDERLYING FEELINGS, AND POSSIBLE SOURCES OF THESE

Some of the young people I have worked with have not wanted to explore past issues that might be impacting on their self-harm. At this point, some people prefer to focus on practical techniques to improve things such as assertiveness, confidence-building, self-esteem, anger management, and/or stress management. However, many do want to explore in a deeper way what lies behind their desire to self-harm. This is where it is easy to become defensive around providing 'informal support', as it doesn't have a clear theoretical approach, unlike counselling or psychotherapy. However, a real strength of the informal support approach is that it can encompass ideas, theories and practice from many sources, and perhaps the key is how I, as a worker, share the responsibility for the process and the work with a young person.

In some ways, it is important for me to monitor, with the young person, whether the informal support is helping. A part of this is for me to be aware of when I might feel that another worker and/or another approach might be of more benefit to the young person. These are arguably the dilemmas faced by anyone working in a therapeutic manner, but informal support builds in this flexibility where other more formal therapeutic approaches may not.

Using certain vehicles, such as sculpts (where objects can be used to represent people) and family trees, has also helped here, especially early on in the process. I see them as simple techniques that allow the young person to get some of their story out of their heads, giving it a more concrete form, by drawing or modelling. Sculpts and family trees also give someone space to reflect on things they might not see in merely describing their relationships (see Case Study 5).

Case Study 5

Julie is a 22-year-old single mum. She wants to work with me in order to find some alternatives to coping with stress. She currently cuts her arms, and although this works, she is increasingly unhappy at seeing it as her only choice in certain stressful situations. As part of her sessions, we talk about her isolation. From this, she agrees that drawing a simple family tree might help both of us get a better idea of how isolated she is. (The idea of a 'sculpt' actually freaks Julie out a bit.)

Julie confidently draws a simple family tree, consisting of Julie and her young son, her brother and her mum and dad (divorced). Through the act of drawing this, Julie ends up spending the next two sessions talking about her difficult relationships with her dad and brother. She is surprised at this, as she always thought that her difficulties were with her mum. Through this process, Julie recognises that her relationship with her mum is actually quite good, but she realises that she is quite dependent on her mum. She begins to see her relationships with her dad and brother as safe because she never asks them for anything. Julie eventually sees that she could take the risk and get support from her dad and brother, and that would in turn take the pressure off the relationship with her mum.

In terms of what these underlying issues might be, by far the most common source that has been identified by young people I've met has been some sort of loss. This has often included bereavement, relationship break-up, or sexual/physical/emotional abuse. Other common aspects have been the on-going effect of past bullying, especially linked to the switch from primary to secondary school. The theme of loss of family structure/security has also been dominant with the young people I have worked with.

A key aspect running throughout this work is to make use of positive aspects of young people and their lives. My fear is that as a practitioner I may be led down a route that is solely problem-based due to the pressures of my own responsibilities. However, I try to take a step away from this, as the positive aspects of a young person's life can provide major evidence and motivation that she/he has the experience and abilities to change things. I guess another way of saying this is that often people's successes can inform their difficulties.

The longer I've been involved with this type of work, the more I've become concerned that the support I can provide may help individuals in a myriad of ways, but has little impact on the cultural and structural issues that contribute greatly to the underlying pressures that give rise to their self-harm. This has led me to become more involved in group activities, where young people can link in with other people who may have similar issues, or at least can be sympathetic because of their own experiences. In particular, facilitating a men-only group using the Social Action model has provided some balance to the limitations of one-to-one work (see Chapter 3 in this book). It is a step away from the individualisation of mental health issues, and an attempt to shift power from organisations and workers to young people.

SUPPORT NEEDS OF WORKERS

The needs of workers are often overlooked in service provision or considered merely as an afterthought. However, I see it as an essential ingredient to consider and resource properly, because it is a direct factor in the provision of adequate support to (young) people who self-harm that is 'healthy' for both the service user and the worker. There is a useful outline to be found in Babiker and Arnold (1997) and a good counselling point of view is discussed by Turp (2003). For example, if I am under pressure to see a range of young people under stress, yet have limited ways of talking about the impact this has on me, it is very likely that this will impact on me personally and also on my practice. One of the main reasons I was attracted to working at 42nd Street was its reputation for a commitment to staff support. This includes peer support, internal and external supervision and group/team supervision.

For me, peer support is the most important. As a community-based worker, I think it is easy to become isolated, so even a five-minute chat with a colleague as we pass in opposite directions can work wonders. Often, these peer support chats are much longer and in-depth, and prove invaluable. There is also the opportunity for ad hoc support from management staff at 42nd Street. Internal supervision with a manager is a good place to explore specific areas of concern, particularly relating to risk. It is also a place to explore coping strategies for dealing with high-stress workloads. I find external supervision really useful for giving me a different perspective on what is happening systemically within 42nd Street.

In addition, group-type support at 42nd Street has proved a really valuable way of reflecting on the work that myself and others carry out with young people. In particular, these arenas have helped me to feel less isolated and more reassured with respect to the emotional impact of working with young people who are suicidal or self-harming. I've felt that my own ways of working have been validated, expanded and challenged within these experiences. In addition, there is something about sharing ideas with a group of co-workers that somehow contributes to cultural and structural shifts in how to respond to the challenges of working with people who are self-harming or suicidal. Also, I find a great source of support and inspiration from art that's relevant to suicide, self-harm and mental health in general (especially music, books and film).

NOT RISKY ENOUGH?

As I have argued, sometimes people who are in high emotional pain, but are considered to be 'low risk', can be denied services they need. If we fail to work with these young people early enough, and if their distress escalates, they may be left to cope with their feelings alone. One of the reasons we fail to work effectively with young people in distress may relate to our own fears. On some level, roles such as mine can embody something about the dominant legal, moral and ethical imperative that is our desperate desire for other people to live *for us, in our way*, be it professionally or personally. We may not be truly listening to the other person's pain, for fear it is in direct competition with the pain we might suffer if they hurt or killed themselves. This fear may make us, unwittingly, push such a person closer to the edge. This is why it is important for us to own and reflect on our own fears, in order to truly connect with others. Working with young people around self-harm can be extremely challenging and immensely rewarding for all involved. I hope my sharing of experiences and reflections will help.

REFERENCES

42nd Street (2003) *Annual Report 2003*. Manchester: 42nd Street.
Babiker, G & Arnold, L (1997) *The Language of Injury: Comprehending self-mutilation*. Leicester: BPS.
Davies, B (2000) *StreetCred? Values and dilemmas in mental health work with young people*. Leicester: National Youth Agency.

Green, K (2001) Finding your own voice: Social Action group work with young people who are suicidal and self-harming. *Youth & Policy, 71,* 59–76.

Indigo Girls (1989) 'Blood and Fire' from the album *Indigo Girls.* Epic Records.

Mental Health Act (1983). London: HMSO.

McDermott, A (1986) *Principles into Practice. A developmental study of a community mental health service.* Manchester: Youth Development Trust.

Pembroke, LR (ed.) (1994) *Self-harm: Perspectives from personal experience.* London: Survivors Speak Out.

Spandler, H (1996) *Who's Hurting Who? Young people, self-harm and suicide.* Gloucester: Handsell Publishing.

Turp, M (2003) Self-harmers: a group apart? *Counselling & Psychotherapy Journal, 14* (5), 6–9.

Chapter 3

FINDING YOUR OWN VOICE: SOCIAL ACTION GROUP WORK WITH YOUNG PEOPLE[1]

KEITH GREEN

INTRODUCTION

This chapter reflects on the experience of running a group for young people at 42nd Street who are suicidal or self-harming. It is written from the group facilitator's viewpoint on a piece of work that attempted to be young person led. It aims to explore and evaluate a youth work approach using a Social Action model. I address issues and dilemmas of empowerment for a group of young people with complex mental health needs and the implications of the work for policies around suicide and self-harm reduction.

SELF-HARM, YOUTH WORK AND SOCIAL ACTION

42nd Street has often dealt with doubts surrounding the validity of a youth work approach to mental health work. In his review of 42nd Street, Davies (2000: 39) describes the inception of the organisation as being:

> Blocked by powerful professional interests ... as mere youth workers based in an unproven voluntary organisation and using informal and open access approaches, they were certainly not to be trusted with the kinds of interventions essential for dealing with mental health problems.

Yet, as argued previously, an informal approach has been central to 42nd Street's provision of group work with young people, and we built on this informal approach in the suicide and self-harm project:

1. An earlier version of this chapter was published in *Youth and Policy*. Green, K (2001) Finding your own voice: Social Action group work with young people who are suicidal and self-harming. *Youth & Policy 71*, 59–76. *Youth & Policy* have agreed for the article to be re-published.

> [S]tarting where young people are starting, including their recreational interests ... unashamedly 'easy going, relaxing and an opportunity for a chat' ... which can often ... look little different from a conventional adolescent leisure programme—albeit with a unique focus on suicide and self-harm. (Davies, 2000: 45)

In planning a new group in 1998, we attempted to retain the informality and accessibility of previous groups and take our thinking around group work further. Our aim was to help young people think about making changes in their lives, rather than just exploring ways of coping with distress and isolation. For example, young people who attended our groups would often express the desire for their feelings or situations to be different, but struggled with knowing how to achieve this. We also aimed to support young people to express their anger in a more productive way. For example, they often expressed anger at their situations or experiences, particularly with the psychiatric system, and would turn this anger inwards, towards themselves. We also tried to minimise the amount of control we retained as workers, as lack of power is a major issue for young people who self-harm. As Spandler (1996: 33) suggests:

> Control ... may be multi-faceted. It may ... mean wanting to keep yourself under control; or being able to do something which other people cannot control; or harming yourself in order to lose control and then come back as a way of getting back into control ... Young people could also lose control when other people tried to 'get in on it' ... by trying to take it away or regulating [self-harm].

A 'Social Action' approach, with its emphasis on the worker as ally, shares many similarities with user/survivor-led movements (for example, the Hearing Voices Network and National Self Harm Network) and the health professionals who have worked alongside them. Thomas (1997: 229) suggests:

> [P]sychiatrists have as much to learn from their patients' accounts of their experiences as they have from their learned professors. Once they appreciate that patients are people who have expertise and skills in their own rights, it may be possible to move into a position where an alliance is possible perhaps by just getting to know about it and/ or talking about it.

We wanted to provide a space where young people could also explore the broader social contexts in which they lived and the experiences which contributed to their distress. It was anticipated that this might help young people to move away from the sense of self-blame they often felt. The Social Action model of group work is a community action model developed over the past twenty plus years (Mullender & Ward, 1991). Mullender and Ward describe 'Social Action' as:

> [A]n effective and empowering vehicle for change ... through resisting labels ... raising awareness ... assisting service users in setting their own agendas for change ... [leading to] the achievement of apparently unattainable goals by individuals previously written off as inadequate and beyond help [with a] 'secondary advantage' of personal change within the group members as well as to the achievement of external change. (1991: 12–13).

The principles of the Social Action model offered a framework to develop the group work. In the planning stages we liaised with the Centre for Social Action (based at the time at De Montfort University, Leicester). Later we worked closely with one of their associates who acted as consultant. The Centre for Social Action (1999: 6) defined the principles of Social Action, summarised as follows:

- All people have skills and understanding, the right to be heard, to define issues facing them, and the right to take action on their own behalf.
- Professionals should not attach negative labels to service users.
- People acting collectively can be powerful so practice should reflect this understanding.
- Individuals in difficulty are often confronted by complex issues rooted in social policy, the environment, and the economy. Responses should also reflect this understanding.
- Methods of working must reflect non-elitist principles and strive to challenge inequality and discrimination.

The model offers a 'process-orientated' framework to help group members explore and find solutions to their personal difficulties. The worker's job is to understand and facilitate this process. The following questions are key to this understanding (the process is not linear as the questions are often returned to).

- WHAT — are your issues, problems and concerns?
- WHY — do these situations exist?
- HOW — can these things be changed?

Embedded in this group process are two key elements. The first element is action. This process recognises young people as social actors and agents for positive change. It understands that young people learn from doing things. What they do may change things, but even if it doesn't, the group has developed tools for dealing with problems in the future. The feeling of empowerment should remain with the group and is the most valuable part of the process. The second is reflection. This is the opportunity for critical reflection, asking what has changed, whether the problems and concerns are still the same, and planning new action by beginning the process again.

THE SUICIDE AND SELF-HARM GROUP

With the planning and preparation process complete, the group ran from December 1998 to May 2000, with a total membership of twenty-three and a core group of around eight. There were more women in the group than men. It was almost exclusively white. The membership had an age range of between 16 and 25. Most had had some contact with psychiatric services or their GP in relation to their mental health problems. This included attendance at Accident & Emergency Departments after self-harming or overdosing, and use of crisis respite services. Most had used, or were using, psychiatric medication. Many had been given some form of psychiatric diagnosis, including personality disorder and schizophrenia.

The group went through a complex process. We explicitly stated our intent at the beginning of the group—that it was about them doing things for themselves and exploring how to make change, however small. The social action process was explained. Youth work games were introduced into the sessions to look at energy, movement, and expressing yourself in ways other than talking. Exercises were initiated to look at the qualities everyone brought to the group; to challenge the negative views of themselves that we knew from experience were often internalised. The idea of collectively working on issues was new for many young people, as they had often experienced an individualised response to their support needs in the past.

In the first two months the group explored what their issues were. Members identified that they often felt ridiculed, judged or dismissed for what they did or felt. They felt their choice to self-harm was often taken away from them by professionals. Some young people talked about having been contracted to stop self-harming, often with the threat that support would be withdrawn if they didn't. Some had a fear of their self-harm, could see no hope and said they really wanted to die. They often felt they were bad or dirty. The men in the group talked of the pressure to be macho. Others talked about how they lacked confidence and a belief in themselves.

When asked why they felt this way, members talked about their experiences earlier in life—of being bullied at school, and of family problems. Some talked of encountering homophobia. There was a long discussion on how they felt GPs, social services, psychiatrists, and schools gave no support with their problems, made them feel like they were wasting the workers' time, or misunderstood them. They felt they were often treated differently because of their age and often told they had their whole life ahead of them, so why should they feel so depressed? Many talked of how they had been labelled—either by psychiatric services (as personality disordered, schizophrenic, attention seeking), or by family or friends (as mad, a nutter, freak, weird, psycho). They debated the usefulness of labels. Some thought diagnoses helped them to be taken seriously, while others felt that they had adopted other people's descriptors of themselves, rather than finding their own words.

The group then moved on to look at how it wanted to tackle some of these issues. They wanted to support each other as a group—sharing their experiences and information, developing their self-belief and confidence. Significantly, the group began to express a desire to move from an individual perspective to exploring more politically motivated action and awareness-raising outside of the group and themselves. This included making demands of psychiatrists, petitioning, producing leaflets, protesting, contacting the media, organising conferences, and even just yelling.

THE ISSUE OF CONTROL: SETTING GROUND RULES

A common concern for professionals in relation to group work with people who self-harm is that it is too risky. As noted by Babiker and Arnold (1997: 113):

> Some workers are wary of allowing people who self-injure to take part in group work together, usually due to concern that members will encourage and copy one another's self-injury.

During the first session of the group, a discussion took place about the advantages and disadvantages of being allowed to self-harm on the premises, which immediately raised the issue of professional attitudes towards risk. After a heated discussion, they decided to have a ground rule permitting them to do this, on the proviso they looked after the wound themselves, and didn't do it in front of other members.

This raised concerns from 42nd Street's managers, who wanted an exploration of what effect this would have on group members, workers, and other young people using 42nd Street. As facilitators, we made it clear we were not going to negotiate on behalf of the group, as our role was to facilitate and support a process that enabled the group to form its arguments and decide what to do—a process that took several weeks.

The group eventually wrote to the managers stating that it was unfair to take away their freedom around this because it made them feel out of control. They felt that the ground rule helped them *not* to self-harm. The ground rule was important in taking the pressure *off* them, rather than being a licence to self-harm. It enabled them to attend the group when they felt at their lowest and get support, instead of staying at home because they felt like harming themselves.

Members requested a meeting with the managers to discuss the issue further. The group facilitated the discussion and put forward their arguments. Despite the managers' initial reservations and concerns, the powerfulness of the young people's viewpoint eventually persuaded the managers to change their position and allow the ground rule to stay in place. During group sessions, no incidents of self-harm were reported. This process was important in being the first example of the group asking for what they wanted and getting it. Their usual experience, particularly with self-harm, was to be told that it wasn't allowed. This time they were able to successfully challenge what professionals told them to do.

Most importantly, it was an example of group members taking responsibility for their self-harm. In direct relation to the recommendations from Babiker and Arnold (1997: 117) it addressed the 'problem of apparent "contagion" [by] encouraging direct verbal expression of feelings, conflicts and difficulties ... giving [participants] as much say as possible in the circumstances and running of their own environment". In the context of concerns about 'contagion', copying, and irresponsibility (often raised when thinking about group work with people who self-harm) this was an important process for the group and 42nd Street to go through.

COMMUNICATION: SILENCED VOICES

The group spent the next few months exploring its collective voice and sense of collective power. It was a huge task for the facilitators to help the group believe that they had a voice that could be heard (given young people's experiences of feeling silenced in their lives) and more importantly that their voice could make some difference to their lives.

However, there was a tension within the group between an internal voice—a need for the group to discuss their experiences and feelings—and an external voice—making public statements about their issues. The group often complained that during group time, there wasn't enough discussion of suicide and self-harm and their personal experiences around this. They felt that there was too much emphasis on action. However, when the opportunity to talk was provided in response to their request, it was difficult for members to communicate what they wanted. It seemed too exposing and distressing for them, which often resulted in silence. As Babiker and Arnold (1997: 64) state, this degree of 'silence' is not uncommon in work around self-harm or suicidal feelings:

> People who self-injure frequently describe themselves as confused and not very good at communicating painful experiences. It would appear that individuals who are at a disadvantage with regard to verbal fluency are more at risk of being drawn to immediate physical 'solutions' such as self-injury.

This is confirmed by the experience of the Crisis Recovery Unit, a therapeutic community for people who self-harm based at the Maudsley Hospital:

> Many self-harming individuals find verbal communication difficult and consequently use their bodies. We provide a range of alternative means of expression ... including creative writing, creative art, drama therapy. (Crowe & Bunclark, 2000: 51)

Similarly, the group began to explore creative ways of expressing themselves. The members tried to write a play based on their experiences, make a video and audio tape of their views; they wrote a group poem and used drama techniques and role-play to put their views across. The use of creative techniques resulted in some powerful and positive expressions of their issues, but the group would often see the use of these techniques as play and talking as the 'real' work. However, as the group progressed they embraced 'playing' far more and it started to become part of their collective voice.

Ideas about performing in public developed. However, the group felt scared of doing this. A dynamic evolved around a lack of safety in the external world as opposed to the group, where they did feel safe to express themselves on some level. Alongside this fear, ran an anger at how they had been treated—an anger which often remained internal. We also explored how this anger could be externalised. In working with this, we literally did ask direct questions such as 'how are people *out there* going to know what life is like for you?' We would then reflect upon how the members' usual response seemed to be to sit at home depressed and remain inactive. At times we had to push the group to believe that this group *could* be different, and that they *could* do things to change how they are treated.

At the beginning of the group, one young woman said that she liked our idea of collectivity. However, what she liked about it was that it presented the possibility that it could collectivise her (and possibly some other members') desire to kill themselves—a chance to form a 'suicide pact'. This obviously shocked us as workers. We worked with this carefully. We ensured we took the distress seriously, whilst not overreacting. We emphasised the aims of the group and the possibility of using the group to achieve change in some other way. We had to work hard in this early stage of the group to help the young people turn these very negative and self-damaging ideas around, and to use this energy for other purposes.

Using this energy was not without its problems. Notably conflict arose for members about how to express themselves, or how to make change, combined with the depressed feelings they were often struggling with. This often had the potential for them to feel as if they had failed, or as though they were under pressure to achieve. This raised feelings of guilt for the facilitators, when being confrontational with a group of depressed young people, and feelings of frustration if the group members were finding it difficult to express themselves.

IDENTITY: VICTIMS OR EXPERTS?

Members' identities as young people with mental health problems were actively challenged. For some, a different perspective on the negative messages they had been given in life was difficult to accept. We often noted that they felt that the cause of their problems was something inherent in them, or an illness—messages that often seemed to have been internalised from an early age. If they let go of this identity then what did this ultimately mean? Members engaged in a process that challenged their beliefs in their own capabilities, skills and qualities, and attempted to value these and empower themselves in utilising them.

Members often expressed their difficulty with this idea by showing a lack of motivation or a resistance to working. They often expressed their fear of change, and looked to the facilitators for answers or direction. A group member expressed that their silence was often as a result of having authority figures (us, the facilitators) in the room. We also realised there was an issue of us, as facilitators, holding a degree of responsibility that wasn't useful—often just by being there. A turning point came when we decided to outline what tasks they had identified and then leave the room so that the members could work on their own, without us. This seemed to work as tasks became more easily achieved.

Leaving the group to work alone provided a powerful message to the young people that they could be left alone, as they had often experienced attitudes that said they weren't responsible enough, or wouldn't be able to cope on their own.

For the facilitators too, it challenged messages about the identity or roles workers often adopt (that of rescuer, or being the problem solver). This could often feel particularly difficult as we were working with people who are perceived as very 'damaged'. Instead, our role here was to facilitate and support a process, but not to act for the young people themselves. As Mullender and Ward (1991: 11) state:

> Practitioners ... are challenged to combine their own efforts with those of oppressed groups without colonising them ... in the place of the customary 'we know best' of traditional practice.

Facilitators had to constantly challenge their need for control. This made the work very challenging, frustrating and at times uncomfortable, in combination with young people's motivation and communication difficulties. These feelings often mirrored those of psychiatrists, nurses and GPs, which young people had often described to us—that they got angry, frustrated and impatient with their patients around their self-harm.

In feeling on an edge of these feelings, consultancy sessions helped the facilitators to reflect upon their own personal process and sense of congruence. It helped us keep the group's real achievements and positive qualities in sight, while constructively challenging and motivating the group, as well as balancing our own expectations with the young people's experience of distress and depression.

THE GROUP TAKES ACTION

With increased confidence, young people began to walk out into the world and make their statements, attending a demonstration in London to stop child sexual abuse, and putting on a stall at a World Mental Health Day event in Manchester.

The 'Stop Child Sexual Abuse' demonstration, organised by a coalition of survivor-led organisations, proved to be an empowering experience. Group members made their own banners, and defiantly marched through central London with hundreds of others. Some group members went on stage at the rally, and talked openly about their experiences of abuse and the confidence that attending the demonstration had given them. The young people described it as a moving and powerful experience for them, particularly as their abuse was so difficult to talk about.

The World Mental Health Day event involved group members contacting the organisers, planning and making displays, setting up a stall in a local market, and talking to members of the public who attended. Again they felt this was a success. During the course of the event one professional asked the group to provide training for their team on self-harm. Another asked whether he could use some of their poems to display in a local day centre. The stall had been more difficult than the demonstration, as it had taken place in Manchester, and not provided the same level of anonymity.

These two pieces of action presented an opportunity for the group to reflect upon what they had done. What was it like to have shouted out their slogans and carried placards demanding the end of child sexual abuse? Did it feel different to externalise their feelings about this rather than internalise them or blame themselves? How did it feel to be visible as survivors of abuse instead of feeling ashamed and hidden away, and what was it like to do this with hundreds of other people.

Responses to these questions included an expression of their feelings of safety due to the support they got from each other, and that the anonymity of being in London had helped them to feel stronger. Most of them said that the effects of being on the demonstration had reached into their lives in Manchester, and they had continued to feel this strength for a few days afterwards.

RAISING AWARENESS

Following these events, the group felt more confident and agreed that it would be good to develop some of their original ideas into an awareness day about suicide and self-harm for professionals and other young people, with workshops, talks and displays. The group spent six months devising, and working towards the day, which went ahead in April 2000.

The displays for the awareness day related to suicide and self-harm, but also reflected their ability to lead very ordinary lives. Their posters showed that they too could be, in their words, 'sexy and cool', that they enjoyed watching football, that they did voluntary work, and were able to draw and write poetry. The day also demonstrated that they could run workshops, speak as experts with professionals and not be seen as victims.

The Suicide and Self-Harm Awareness Day was a major success, with over thirty professionals, students and young people attending. The group put on workshops looking at relaxation, art therapy, and treatment at Accident & Emergency departments. A play about suicide and self-harm was performed which ended with a question-and-answer session. Most importantly the group members planned and facilitated the whole day without any help from us as workers. The young people produced their own report about the Awareness Day, which illustrated the sense of planning, achievement and worth that the group members felt before and after the day (42nd Street, 2000: 3):

> This is a rare opportunity for us to get our views across because it was done by us, the people who experience suicide and self-harm in our lives. We could tell people what it is really like for us and what help we really need. All we want is to be listened to and not told who we are and what we need. A little understanding goes a long way.

After the Awareness Day, we announced that, as facilitators, we would be ending our involvement with the group soon, due to other circumstances. The last weeks of the group combined both a reflection on the whole experience of the group and an airing of members' dissatisfaction with the group ending. Discussions took place about the idea of them facilitating the group themselves. There were some doubts about this, but the discussions showed a newfound confidence, maturity, and belief in their abilities. Alongside this they also expressed disillusionment and anger at 42nd Street for not providing a new worker to carry on the group.

Reflecting on the group itself, members talked about how they had gained more confidence and felt an increased sense of personal power. Some reflected that they no longer felt that psychiatrists were 'God', and that they were no longer scared to stand up for themselves. One person talked about how he felt able to cry again, and that it had been useful to be able to have been both happy and sad within the group. Another described it as the place where she could 'breathe'. One member movingly drew two pictures—one of a large figure talking down to a little figure, and next to that, a drawing of two equal-sized figures talking to each other, with the caption 'Me at home before I came to the group … Me at home now'.

Significant questions were being asked by the young people of themselves during this time. Issues of group commitment, location, safety, and leadership were discussed and whether they felt able and confident enough to take charge of the group. Facilitators also posed serious questions of 42nd Street's 'culture' in terms of an overprotective streak coupled with practical barriers that thwarted young people accessing resources directly. Would a group of young people meet on their own, something that had never happened before in its twenty-year history?

Members developed their thinking about these issues and requested that 42nd Street's managers allow them the use of premises to run the group. The managers agreed, but wanted a worker to oversee this. Unfortunately no worker was available to do this. After discussion, the young people in the group decided it would be too difficult to continue. The members ended the group with a social event, with an emphasis on valuing the qualities they had all shown over the past eighteen months.

CONCLUSIONS—IMPACT, DEVELOPMENT AND IMPLICATIONS

The group had achieved a great deal over the past 18 months and there was a sense of internal change in many of the young people—an ability to express themselves differently and a willingness to take on leading roles in the work they were involved in. This increased self-confidence and sense of self-worth affected broader, external change—particularly through the Awareness Day. Some of the professionals attending the day spoke of how the young people's presentations would affect their practice in future.

However, the longer-term effects of being involved in the group process are more difficult to assess. Many of the young people have moved on from 42nd Streets' services (several of them have gone on to attend college or have become involved in voluntary work). Some young people have also continued to experience distressing times and have continued to use psychiatric services.

Within the consultancy sessions, group facilitators reflected that, ideally, there was a need for the group to have gone through the Social Action process again. If they had had the opportunity to explore again what their issues and concerns were, and how they could affect some difference to these, then the group may have strengthened their learning and consolidated the sense of change they were beginning to feel.

However, it is important to remind ourselves of one of the challenges the Social Action model presented to us as workers—that we can play a different role as facilitators than that of 'rescuer' or 'problem solver'. The group too, should not be seen as the answer to all the young people's problems.

However powerful the experience of the group was, ultimately all we could do was work alongside these young people in exploring some different options to the ones they had already explored. They could take from that process what felt useful for them.

What emerges from the evaluation of practice is an argument that an informal and accessible youth work-based approach can be effective in working with young people who are self-harming or suicidal. Experiences of previous group work; looking at coping strategies, attempting to reduce isolation, building relationships with young people and helping them to do that with each other (however valuable that may be)—suggest not all forms of group work are robust enough to help young people to achieve a sense of change and purpose.

What was needed in developing this group work was a clearly defined model that had explicit beliefs in the power young people can have and act upon. The Social Action model offers a means to explore more purposeful work with young people alienated from traditional mental health responses to these issues. The model enables a group of young people, who are often perceived as unable to take responsibility or control, and in need of or beyond treatment, in a more effective way than we had previously achieved. However, the tensions between taking action and the young people's need to talk about their feelings required constant attention.

As demonstrated in this chapter, emancipatory group work can highlight tensions, conflicts and challenges for workers and young people that require a sophisticated response. It is vital that funders and agencies ensure that this work is structurally supported. It was only with internal supervision, and external consultancy that took seriously the emotional demands of suicide and self-harm work and the challenges of working in the way we did, that we were able to work effectively.

For funders of health services and policy makers, the lessons are two-fold. First, there is a need to value a non-medicalised approach, combined with an understanding of the social contexts affecting young people. The youth work basis and emancipatory nature of this piece of work has demonstrated that it can engage young people who find it difficult to find value in traditional medical responses. Our practice asked important questions of the young people about the feelings and experiences that lay underneath the symptoms of their distress, and encouraged them to look at the broader social contexts they live in and the effects these may have upon their mental health.

Second, services need to ask questions about dominant attitudes towards young people who are self-harming or suicidal. As demonstrated by the experience presented in this chapter, mental health practitioners, service providers and policy makers, must recognise that effective working with young people is best achieved by an openness to challenge around the identities and labels we give to young people and the powerful positions we hold as workers. Young people need to identify for themselves what their needs are and the framework in which those needs can be met. Asking these questions and working alongside young people in implementing the answers for themselves is the crux of effective practice with young people alienated from mainstream mental health services.

REFERENCES

42nd Street Suicide and Self-Harm Group (2000) *Awareness Day Report.* Manchester: Unpublished.

Babiker, G & Arnold, L (1997) *The Language of Injury—Comprehending self-mutilation.* London: BPS Books.

Centre for Social Action (1999) *Centre for Social Action Review 1994–1999.* Leicester: De Montfort University.

Crowe, M & Bunclark, J (2000) Repeated self-harm and its management. *International Review of Psychiatry, 12,* 48–53.

Davies, B (2000) *StreetCred? Values and dilemmas in mental health work with young people.* London: Youth Work Press.

Mental Health Foundation (1999) *Bright Futures: Promoting children and young people's mental health.* London: Mental Health Foundation.

Mullender, A & Ward, D (1991) *Self-Directed Groupwork: Users take action for empowerment.* London: Whiting and Birch.

Spandler, H (1996) *Who's Hurting Who? Young people, self-harm and suicide.* Manchester: 42nd Street.

Thomas, P (1997) *The Dialectics of Schizophrenia.* London: Free Association Books.

Chapter 4

SUPPORTIVE COMMUNITIES AND HELPFUL PRACTICES: THE CHALLENGE FOR SERVICES

IAN MURRAY

When life is unkind and we injure ourselves, we will often have scars. If the surgeon cuts us open, the scars are a visible reminder of pain and recovery. Similarly, when something horrible happens to us, we carry the experience and its scars with us as a careful reminder and an example to learn from. Trauma creates psychological scars. The consequences of surviving repeated and sustained trauma, that we cannot control or stop, are long term. We learn to survive these experiences in ways that are both perplexing and frustrating if we are on the outside, and startling and disturbing if we are on the inside. These consequences, often traumatic in themselves, are the internal manifestation of scarring from the trauma survived. The act of self-harm, for whatever personal reason, often results in scars on the outside. People who deliberately harm themselves have become more open with us than before. There is no doubt that the changes in attitude towards abuse in recent years have made disclosure less difficult.

The rise in self-help projects for younger people have created forums where issues such as self-harm can be discussed in relative safety. 42nd Street is one of the forerunners in this approach. I encountered 42nd Street when I and my colleagues, Linda Langton and Kate Roberts, were asked to work with them in delivering two conferences on young people who self-harm (Murray, 1998). 42nd Street approached us, as we were travelling along similar paths and they had heard of the work we were doing at the time and our approach to self-harm. There were members of the user group on the conference working party, so I got to know some of them. My enduring impression of these young people, whose average age was about 18 years, was how open and relaxed they were about their self-harm. I was able to talk with them, not only about their experience, but also about their views on how a service for self-harming individuals should work. They were clear, forthright and unafraid. I was extremely impressed. They were relatively untouched by conventional psychiatry and so had thus far avoided the ardour of dismissive paternalism. This was refreshing to see. I was moved by them and felt grateful because it validated ways of working that had made sense to me.

My interest in self-harm came about in the early 1980s when I was a nurse, managing a psychiatric hostel in Lisburn, Northern Ireland. It was an unusual situation in that it was comprised of five houses in the middle of a council estate. I lived in one of the houses and fifteen residents lived in the other four. I was the only member of staff apart from a part-time domestic. I worked there for nine years, living on site for the first four years with my wife and two small sons.

There were two young girls living in one of the hostel houses. Linda (17 years old) and Ellen (18 years old).[1] They had been sharing the house for a few weeks and had seemed to settle in, until one evening when I was watching television having finished for the day and the doorbell rang. It was Linda in an excited state. She wanted me to come quickly and see Ellen who had locked herself in the bathroom. Linda said there was blood coming from under the door. She hadn't exaggerated; there was what seemed like an enormous amount of blood coming from under the door. I asked Ellen to open the door but she would not answer. Eventually, I had to let myself in. Once inside, I was able to see that the damage was less than I feared but Ellen needed sutures. She was in a state of subdued distress. I asked her if she minded if I dressed her wounds and she agreed. I brought her over to my house and covered her wounds sufficiently for her to travel in my car to the casualty department. Linda was back on the front doorstep and wanted to accompany her friend. I noticed what I had missed the first time. Linda was dripping blood on my step as she had cut her wrists as well.

As both girls had been placed by a psychiatric hospital, convention dictated that my response to their behaviour should have been to re-admit them. We discussed this on the way to casualty in the car. Linda and Ellen clearly liked living in the hostel and they both felt that admission to hospital would be unhelpful. It appeared that Ellen's distress was more to do with how she expected me to respond than about the act of self-harm. She was drawing on her previous experiences where the consequences of her self-injury often meant she had to bear anger and sanctions from hospital staff. My own experience of working in the hospitals left me in no doubt as to what she feared. Periods of self-harm would often result in prolonged suicide watches, the removal of all sharp objects, the restriction of ward privileges and movement. Staff were often hostile and felt let down by the 'breach of trust' inherent in the act. It was often a confusing and fraught period. The girls and I agreed that after getting them patched up, we would all go back to the hostel and pick up where we left off. After all they had trusted me and it

---

1. Linda and Ellen are pseudonyms to protect client identity, as are the others mentioned later in the text.

seemed only right to return the favour. Shortly after we returned home, there was yet another ring on the bell. Outside stood Linda and Ellen with a mop and bucket. They had come to clean the step.

Ellen disappeared shortly after that and I lost contact, but Linda stayed with me for a further two years and was joined by her brother and sister, all victims of the same trauma and abuse. There were other episodes of self-harm with all three, but having made the decision, I continued to 'pick up the pieces' and each of the siblings made the uneasy transition into adulthood intact. Linda's sister Mary married a soldier and I substituted for the bride's father at the wedding and also took the photographs. Her brother Alan joined the police and is now married with children. He had reached sergeant when I last met him. Linda is now in her early 40s and has three teenage children of her own. Occasionally we would meet, and she would remind me, with a wry smile, of the day she cleaned my step.

In 1993, I commissioned and managed Dryll y Car, an eight-bed unit in the statutory sector, with the distinction of having a policy of non-judgement and promoting safer self-harm. The unit staff understood that self-harm was impossible to police and pointless to criticise or punish. With the backing of our consultant psychiatrist, Philip Thomas, we permitted self-harm to happen on the unit as part of an agreement with the service user that included agreeing to disclose any self-harm immediately after the event and to follow sensible precautions like using clean blades (Thomas, 1998). The staff would help repair the damage and would always, where necessary, escort and support service users who had to attend casualty. This strategy was underpinned by the conviction that self-harm was a way of surviving a trauma that lurked below the surface.

In addition to the support and trust we fostered, we offered therapy. We discovered that the self-harmer's readiness to do this depended on a couple of things. The person's internal progress, or lack of it, in dealing with whatever manifested itself, was a major factor. Equally important was the stage of trust we had achieved, as weighed against the service user's bad experiences in the past in other NHS settings. Mostly, we offered support and the opportunity for reciprocity. Without support, therapy is at best a first aid measure. A useful illustration is the mending of a broken cup. 'Therapy' is the careful piecing together of the parts to make the cup whole again. The 'support' is the glue that holds the pieces together and allows the cup to be functional again. Clearly the 'therapy' will not work without 'support' and it is the 'support' that maintains functionality and ultimately helps people.

BEING HELPFUL

Even though self-harm and attempted suicides are problems faced by psychiatric professionals daily, it is more common for them to behave in an unhelpful way than a helpful one. This is not to say that the professional does not *want* to be helpful. More often he/she does not know how to respond or has fallen for the myths of 'attention seeking behaviour'. The tradition of professionalism has as an adjunct, a belief that is rooted in paternalism—a sure knowledge that what they believe to be right *is* actually right. Professional responses and interactions are often guided by this belief. This is a major obstacle in the path to being helpful. Helpfulness comes from two places that act as a counterbalance to the professional view.

Firstly, it comes from knowing where the boundaries of our expertise are and recognising the value of the user's experience. Power is always a vexing problem in the debate surrounding psychiatry. The truth is that power is a latent energy that exists in us all. We can choose to exercise it or not. Often others influence us into believing that we cannot do so. They try to convince us that we should be subject to their power. The power interaction between the psychiatric professional and the service user is undoubtedly biased towards the professional, as the 'whole person', 'the expert', 'the carer', the person with *responsibility* for the service user and, by no means least, the person vested with the power of legislation over the service user.

Like the service user, our 'wholeness' is only apparent when compared alongside the deeper disintegration of others. We ourselves are not entirely whole and appear less so than others more complete than us. Our 'expertise' consists of many morsels of our and others' experience and a few theoretical tools. Our 'expertise' spreads thinly on someone else's bread. We cannot claim to be experts in someone else's life. The most emancipating experience of our lives is the understanding of our limitations. Understanding our boundaries allows us to work to our potential within them. Only when we understand this are we free to help. Often we, as workers, have contributed further to the misery of sufferers by placing unreasonable demands on them and by believing too much in our expertise and not enough in service user's opinions and experiences.

The second factor in helpfulness is accepting that being helpful is a position we take, on the understanding that the recipient may want to respond by returning the favour. The problem we have in *providing* support is that we make certain assumptions about the 'rules' of supportiveness and, to create support services, ignore the essential ingredients that make support a recipe for success. Support is not a service, it is a position in life. We take the position of either being supportive or being supported. The mechanisms of support, the goals we set and the parameters that surround the support are secondary to the position.

Implicit in taking a supportive position, or a supported position, are three understandings. Firstly, we must understand that either position is voluntary and subject to choice. We can choose to be supportive or not to be supportive; equally we can choose to accept or not accept support. To adopt a supportive position suggests that we care about the person and value them. To simply *provide* support ignores this position and creates disempowerment and dependency.

The second understanding is the necessity of maintaining the supported person's view of their own worth. The person elects to be supported with the unspoken understanding that they trust the other person to give the support they need at that point. Having made the choice also demonstrates an understanding of their worthiness to be supported. Being supportive within this understanding reinforces the supported person's self-appraisal of intrinsic worth.

The third understanding is an extension of the second and is a benchmark for the total concept of support. In a supportive relationship there is a tacit understanding that reciprocities can exist and that there is potential for the supportive roles to be reversed at a later time. These potentials are the foundation of personal worth for the supportee. To explicitly deny the opportunity for reciprocity to the supported person is a fundamental breach of society's most basic rule. It implies unworthiness on their part and denies them the basic mechanism of recovery. The relationship is at best a supportive-looking type of consumer/provider interaction and the worst possibility is the creation of dependency along with a strong message decrying their value in society.

Like all other needs, the response to self-harm and suicide risk might benefit from a basic recipe that allows more helpful things to occur. The challenge for today's professional is to build some foundations for helpfulness. They need to understand that the road to recovery requires the service user to follow society's rules and exercise skill in creating the reciprocities required for them to survive. This compels the worker to see that there can only be one set of rules for everyone if recovery is to be possible. In order to do this we need to challenge some of the fundamental values that have their beginnings in Victorian times.

WHO DESERVES HELP?

In the Victorian age, the poorhouse, or workhouse, was devised as a means of dealing with the impoverished of the parish. Being 'on the parish' was the last step before destitution. Many argued that it was the same thing. Parish councils functioned as benefactors to poor families by offering handouts to those considered deserving. Those who were undeserving were consigned to the workhouse or left to beg. The parish council, led by the minister, made the decision of worth. Worth was often decided on moral or religious grounds. A regular church attender was considered more worthy, for example, than a non-attender. The morally pure were seen as more worthy than the morally delinquent.

This idea of the deserving and undeserving poor serves to illustrate how we are capable, even in the most benevolent of situations, of making prejudicial judgements. Those of us who use self-harm for dealing with distress often find themselves in the role of the undeserving when they seek help from professionals.

We need to look at our relationship with those who self-harm in an attempt to highlight the problems of professional perceptions and the influence this has on how we practise. Then we can make the shift from the old Parish paternalism to an approach that respects the sufferer's experience and shows a willingness to work with the self-harmer on their terms. That we do this is of paramount importance, particularly for the younger group of self-harmers, so that they avoid being forced into the challenging behaviour characteristic of so many of their elder counterparts to which we have contributed by our actions. The rise in our awareness of young people who self-harm requires that we take special care not to repeat the mistakes of the past and that we take the opportunity to listen, support and form good alliances with them from the outset. It is through the process of seeking common ground that we get to understand our own ground and that of our potential ally.

Self-harm can be upsetting to observe, more difficult still to understand. When you look at self-harm in comparison to other risky behaviours, it is instructive to note the difference in how society views the two types of behaviour and how it makes value judgements on both kinds of behaviour. Occupations where the risk of self-harm is very high are not only sanctioned but are also valued as areas in which to exercise individual choice. Climbing a mountain or saving someone from a fire is seen to be desirable behaviour involving self-control or self-sacrifice. The exercise of this choice is seen to be a rational act. The attractiveness of 'living on the edge' can be seen clearly in the Pepsi Max advert where the young men are seen base jumping and living life 'to the max'.

Young people who intentionally harm themselves are viewed negatively because they appear to have little control over what happens. In addition, the scars are visible in some form. It is considered irrational, with the consequence that those who engage in the behaviour are castigated for their lack of self-control. This, together with the popular misconception that the act of self-harm carries with it suicidal intent, can result in those who self-harm being reviled, accused, neglected and abused in casualty departments, GP practice surgeries, psychiatric outpatient clinics and inpatient units (Coleman et al., 1997; Pembroke et al., 1998; Smith, 1998). This needs to change.

When we suffer from cancer, the doctors give us toxic cocktails of drugs to help us survive. If we hurt inside they may use knives to cut us. These strategies are the acceptable cost of our struggle to survive. It seems strange to me that when people use self-harm for the same reasons it is viewed so negatively. While self-harming behaviour is a visible manifestation of the person's pain, it is really an intervention against that pain and not a symptom. To be able to effectively help with the problems underlying self-harm, we must first learn to distinguish the symptoms from the attempts to relieve them.

Most people enter the mental health professions with the intent to 'cure'. They believe, reasonably, that there are curative skills to be acquired. Most service users also share the belief that professionals can cure. With time, the limits become obvious to both worker and service user, and motivation turns to frustration. The usual outcome of this is that the worker who maintains the paternalistic belief that he/she is right begins to blame the service user for the lack of success. As noted before, we are not experts in the lives of others. Trying to be so is the foot that trips us up.

THE CHALLENGE FOR STATUTORY SERVICES

We, as human beings, are governed by feelings. As professionals, we are encouraged to ignore or suppress our feelings when dealing with another's distress. Yet we intuitively apply feelings to every situation, person, experience and interaction. Acknowledgement of our subjective side aids and informs our understanding and helps us to recognise our own underlying beliefs and biases. We cannot expect to understand the distress of another if we suppress our subjective side. All positive practice has its beginnings in an ethos that is, in turn, determined by values. They are the engine that drives vision and purpose.

Most interventions with people who self-harm lack vision. The purpose of the interactions is muddied by bias. You might be forgiven for thinking that 'cutting contracts' and unsympathetic behaviour in casualty departments and in GP surgeries are purposeful interventions. They are, *if* your purpose is to create conflict and drive the problem underground. The truth is that such strategies are stressful for everyone concerned and have been shown for years to be ineffective.

'Cutting contracts' are based on behaviourist theory. They are also reminiscent of the 'ducking stool' approach. The self-harmer agrees not to self-harm while he/she is an inpatient on the ward or while being seen by a therapist, in return for therapeutic interventions designed to reduce the need for self-harming behaviour and possibly other rewards. While this approach has had some limited success, users who have been subject to such contracts complain that the professional often fails to come up with a useful alternative, or to address the underlying problem, resulting in the user's return to self-harm. This breaches the 'cutting contract'. The consequence for the user is withdrawal of therapy and often discharge from hospital.

The message that self-harming behaviour is a way of coping with distress is lost in the cutting-contract scenario, which is short-sighted in the belief that if you can stop the behaviour, you can resolve the problem. The need to self-harm is underpinned by the need to survive. Understanding this is an essential precursor to effective interventions that do not judge either the behaviour or the person. People who self-harm do so because they feel it is the most effective way of dealing with their pain. They are placing trust in us to understand and support them when they seek our help. The approach of those who work in casualty departments and psychiatric wards can affect the attitude and often the future lives of such people. It is important for all people who hurt themselves that their experience of us as professionals is not dismissive, paternal or patronising. If it is, the service user will challenge us. This is the beginning of the kind of bad experiences that inevitably lead to many of the difficult and challenging encounters later on. Unfortunately, the persistent professional reductionist belief begins to pathologise these encounters and the service user's challenge becomes evidence for 'personality disorder' which automatically blames the behaviour on the service user and creates an underclass of 'the undeserving' mentioned before.

Survivors of self-harm often feel challenged or judged by professionals. These perceived attitudes of professionals can provoke defensive and challenging behaviour in response. The service user acquires the label 'attention seeking' or 'troublemaker'. Young people particularly tend to be more intense and questioning. These questions should be encouraged and not suppressed. We should take the challenges seriously and rise to meet them in a positive manner. Shabby treatment deserves challenging. If we accept that, apart from the 'nimby-ism' (not in my back yard) of 'cutting contracts', we can do little to prevent the act of self-harm, and realising the boundaries of our ability to change this, we can then concentrate our efforts into looking at ways to really help.

While there will be debate over areas of safe practice, there is no doubt that working cooperatively with people who harm themselves creates trust and allows the pain to be explored together. One challenge is to overcome our fears of risk-taking and to develop an informed and imaginative approach to the handling of risk. Management support for intelligent risk-taking in this kind of practice must be explicit from the outset. It is their responsibility to ensure that good skills and strategies are in place to enable an effective response. The ultimate challenge is to evaluate the risk and have the courage to take it. There is certainly a high risk of suicide, not least through the frequency of self-harm and through misadventure. Those risks already exist but cooperation, trust and education in harm reduction can substantially reduce them.

The National Self Harm Network (NSHN) took the lead in setting out ways of developing services for people who self-harm by educating professionals in better attitudes and strategic interventions. Its work is strongly influenced by survivors of self-harm and their experience of treatment by professionals. The consequence should be that young people who present to services would elicit a more helpful professional response (Pembroke et al., 1998). The NHS has a responsibility to respond constructively to this and there are four areas in which action would improve the situation.

1. RAISING MENTAL HEALTH PROFESSIONALS' AWARENESS AND KNOWLEDGE OF SELF-HARM

While not all forms of self-harm result in emergency care, a significant minority of those, particularly those who cut themselves, end up in casualty departments or GP practices. If workers take a more positive attitude to self-harm, more people who do it will come forward for assistance without fear of judgement (Pembroke et al., 1998). Organisations like the NSHN provide workshops for casualty staff but this should be extended to the speciality of mental health and aimed at ward managers, nursing staff and psychiatrists. It is important that managers recognise the contribution to be made by service users in this area and budget for this.

2. DEVELOPMENT OF SELF-HELP AND SAFE HOUSES FOR PEOPLE WHO HARM THEMSELVES

Acute admission units do not provide an appropriate environment for someone who self-harms. Information that is more systematic is required about the experiences of people who self-harm on these units. Anecdotally, this makes grim reading, but we have to start by establishing what sort of support people who self-harm want at point of crisis, with traditional acute provision perhaps being complimented by smaller community-based houses offering crisis support. It is crucial that those who purchase and provide services see the need to pay particular attention to young people who self-harm and provide approaches based on the significant contribution of groups like 42nd Street. There really is no alternative if we want to avoid the mistakes of the past.

3. Reducing the dangers of self-harm

In medicine, there is a well-established tradition in which patients are encouraged to accept responsibility for their own treatment. Diabetic clinics have specialist nurses to train patients in self-management. Of course this is different from harm minimisation but public health medicine has established a precedent for this. Casualty staff, liaison nurses, GPs and practice nurses should get extra training in encouraging safer self-harm. This should include information about less dangerous ways of cutting so as to reduce the risk of damaging blood vessels, tendons and nerves, care of wound sites and the avoidance of infection. Dressing and suture packs should be available for those who want to care for their wounds themselves or with the help of friends and supporters.

4. Creating posts for user practitioners and specialist advocates

There are many examples countrywide of people with backgrounds as service users being employed on community treatment teams. This has proven to be a great opportunity to inject a level of understanding previously impossible to achieve. As self-harm is a significant problem that is compounded by our lack of ability to understand it and respond effectively, we should consider tapping into such a wealthy source. The inclusion of specialist workers/advocates in liaison teams would be a great start. These ideas require a genuine commitment on the part of politicians, purchasers, GPs, managers and practitioners before the changes can become a reality.

CONCLUSION

We cannot set the timescales for working with young people who self-harm or even determine exactly how it might be undertaken. At best it is often an untidy process. We must learn to work patiently and in close alliance with the service user. We need to value people and their experiences and avoid the pitfalls of deciding whether some are more deserving than others, and to value our limitations along with the self-harmer's contribution. We cannot make a difference alone but we can make a difference together. The need to change is clear and there is already plenty of evidence to support the changes in approach documented in this book: changes that are already benefiting the young self-harmer.

REFERENCES

Coleman, R, Murray, I, Thomas, P & Baker, P (1997) From victims to allies. *Nursing Times 93*, 40–2.

Murray, I (1998) *Why Young People Are Attempting Suicide/Self-Harming: The implications for mental health services*. Keynote speech at Who's Hurting Who? Conference, ORT House, London, 3 September 1998, Pavilion Press/42nd Street.

Pembroke, LR, Murray, I, Lynn, F, Harrison, A & Pacetti, R (1998) Patients who self-harm. *Nursing Times 94*, 36–9.

Smith, M (1998) *Self-Harm: Victim to victor*. Gloucester: Handsell Publishing.

Thomas P (1998) *Deliberate Self-harm and Psychiatry.* Manchester Metropolitan University, April 21. Keynote speech at Self-harm, Abuse and the Psychotic Experience (SHAPE) Conference.

PART TWO:
ABUSE, OPPRESSION AND SELF-HARM

Chapter 5

CALMING DOWN:
SELF-INJURY AS STRESS CONTROL[1]

ROSE CAMERON

Perhaps the most common reason given by people who self-injure is that doing so releases tension and calms them down. This can be, for those who do not self-injure, the most difficult to understand empathically. Injury *causes* tension for most people—we wince and brace ourselves against the pain. People who deliberately injure themselves in order to release tension have the opposite response—they relax and wind down. Subjects taking part in a piece of research into self-injury (Haines et al., 1995) were asked to imagine harming themselves. Those in the group who normally self-injured measurably relaxed whilst they imagined injuring themselves. The 'control' subjects, who did not normally self-injure, did not relax—they became more stressed.

As counsellors, we draw on our own emotional experience—knowing how something has felt for us, or how we imagine it might feel—when empathising with clients. Having experienced something similar, or being able to imagine doing so, enables us to get into the same ball park as our client, and only becomes a problem when we slip into thinking that the client's experience must be the *same* as our own, as opposed to similar. Anger, shame, and the desire to make other people notice us or to feel guilty, are all common human experiences that most of us will feel to some degree at some point in our lives. We therefore have some experience, however slight, to draw upon when trying to empathise with a client who self-harms for these sorts of reasons.

Feeling calmer after a self-inflicted injury is not a universal human experience. Counsellors who have never deliberately injured themselves in order to calm down, and do not calm down at the thought of doing so, will not have their own emotional experience to draw on when trying to empathise with a client who self-harms for this reason. If we do not feel relief at the thought of cutting into our own flesh, we are unlikely to empathise well with someone who does. We can accept that our client's experience is as they say, and that it is different from our own, but this falls short of empathic

---

1. This chapter is adapted from Cameron, R (in press) Working with clients who self-injure. In J Tolan, *Person-centred Practice*. London: Sage.

understanding. However, theoretical understanding can be a source of empathic understanding if it enables us to imagine an experience, and fortunately, there is a wealth of recent research that can help us imagine the relief some people get from injuring themselves.

HYPER-AROUSAL

This body of research, which comes from a number of different disciplines including developmental psychology, neuroscience and biochemistry, has added to our understanding of psychological development, and of psychological damage, by studying pre-verbal infants. It demonstrates that brain development, specifically the right-hand side of the brain, which deals with feelings, and with relationships, is dependent on the quality of our earliest relationship. Babies who are not met with loving and empathic care giving do not become able, as adults, to regulate their own feelings; in other words, they cannot choose to calm down when stressed (Schore, 1994, 2003a, 2003b).

Imagine a very young baby. A baby who is hungry, uncomfortable, scared or in pain. There is little the baby can do about it, other than cry. If its parent (I will use 'parent', although 'care-giver' or 'significant other' would be equally appropriate) is able to empathise accurately and respond to the baby's need for food or a clean nappy, they will feed or change the baby, and soothe it. If the parent does not make psychological contact with the baby by responding to it, or does not respond with accurate and loving empathy, all the baby can do is cry harder.

The baby's face will become distorted with crying, its skin will flush, its whole body will become tense—it will display all the signs of heightened physiological arousal and tension. As the baby becomes stressed, its brain triggers the production of various chemicals including the hormone cortisol (Yehuda, 1999). Cortisol helps us deal more effectively with stressful situations by helping us focus all our resources. It does this by shutting down other systems, like the immune system, and our relaxation and learning processes (Chambers et al., 1999; McEwen, 1999).

If the parent changes the baby's nappy etc., its physical need may be taken care of, but the baby will probably not stop crying unless it is also soothed. Soothing—gentle, loving attention, stroking, patting, gazing, making faces and baby talk—is as important as changing or feeding the baby. It is this embodied interaction that enables the baby's biological process to get into synch with its psychological process (Schore, 2003b). As it is soothed, the baby's cortisol level drops, and its immune, learning and relaxation systems are restored.

If a crying baby is habitually ignored, treated coldly, or not soothed and comforted by being held and patted or stroked, and does not have its needs responded to with empathic understanding, its system becomes flooded with cortisol, and if this happens often, its cortisol receptors, which mop up cortisol, close down. When the baby's cortisol level rises in response to stress in the future, there are not enough receptors to absorb it (Caldji et al., 2000). Cortisol flooding the hippocampus can affect its growth (Lyons et al., 2000). If this happens the child's memory and ability to learn will also be compromised.

Although we are particularly vulnerable to this damage in the hippocampus as babies, cortisol receptors can also close down in adults experiencing long-term stress. Disabled cortisol receptors make the hippocampus less sensitive to cortisol, and this interrupts the process by which it tells the hypothalamus to stop ordering cortisol production. Cortisol levels continue to rise, which can lead to neuron loss in the hippocampus. Just as the neural pathways in a baby's brain may fail to develop because its parent fails to regulate its stress levels through loving and empathic contact, so parts of an adult's brain may atrophy as a result of long-term stress (Collins & Depue, 1992; Konyescsni & Rogeness, 1998).

So, too much cortisol that stays around for too long is really bad news. It is important that we are able to calm down, and when we are very young, this is a surprisingly complicated business. A baby's biological and psychological stress responses do not work in harmony with each other—it cannot 'tell' its body to calm down just because the emergency is over. As every parent knows, simply offering a really distressed baby milk, or changing its nappy is not enough. The baby needs to be held, stroked, looked at, talked to—it cannot calm down by itself. Even if the baby's physical need for food or a clean nappy has been met, it cannot reduce its physiological arousal (flushed skin, tense body, etc.) without help (Gunnar & Donzella, 2002).

It is the embodied and relational process of soothing—stroking, patting, kissing, eye contact, playing with sound—that enables our physiological and psychological processes to work in harmony with each other. Unless this process happens often enough between the baby and parent, the baby's mind and body do not start to work in relation to each other, and the baby becomes an adult who cannot calm down just because the emergency is over (Schore 1994, 2003a, 2003b).

So, imagine feeling really stressed about something, and what it would be like to do whatever normally works for you—rationalising, talking about how you feel to someone who can really understand, working out a strategy and so on—but for it to just not make a difference to how wound up you feel. Imagine this always being the case. Imagine being simply unable to calm down.

WHY SELF-INJURY WORKS

Although a great many people who self-harm say that they do so to relieve stress, research into the relationship between self-injury and stress reduction is scant. However, the research there is (Sachsse et al., 2002; Haines et al., 1995) indicates that self-harm is, for some people, an effective means of reducing physiological stress.

Research into who self-injures is more plentiful, and shows that it is usually the quality of the emotional relationship between a child and its main carer that determines who will, and who will not, self-harm later in life (van der Kolk et al., 1991; Linehan, 1993). People who self-injure are very likely to have been emotionally abused or neglected as children; to have suffered a significant separation from their main carer or to have been ignored or responded to in an invalidating rather than empathic way. Even monkeys who are parted from their mothers self-injure. Although a great many people who deliberately injure themselves have had extreme and obviously traumatic experiences, such as physical or sexual abuse, many people who have been sexually or physically abused do not self-injure. Van der Kolk et al. (1991: 1669) conclude that,

> [N]eglect came to be the most the most powerful indicator of self-destructive behaviour. This implied that although childhood trauma contributes heavily to the initiation of self-destructive behaviour, lack of secure attachments maintains it.

This strongly suggests, in the light of the neurological research summarised earlier, that people whose earliest relationship was insecure and who self-injure have a biological stress response that is out of synch with their psychological process, and over which they do not have the degree of control that is usual for other people.

Although research into the effects of self-injury is scant, the little research done so far suggests that self-harm does indeed reduce stress. The authors of a study that showed cortisol levels being raised prior to an incident of self-injury, and lowered for some days afterwards, conclude that:

> ... self-mutilating behaviour may be regarded as an unusual but effective coping strategy for the self-regulation of hyper-arousal and/ or dissociative states and for gaining control over an otherwise uncontrollable stress response. (Sachsse et al., 2002: 672)

The authors of another study (Haines et al., 1995), notice a time lag between self-harmers showing a decrease in biological arousal (heart rate, pulse etc.), and saying that they felt better. They conclude that 'this result suggests that it is the alteration of psychophysiological arousal that may operate to reinforce and maintain the behaviour, not the psychological response,' (ibid: 481). In other words, self-injury reduces physiological stress first, and this seems to be why people do it. I have certainly worked with clients who have said that although they still felt bad after injuring themselves, at least it was 'calm bad'.

The research so far suggests that self-harm is also self-maintenance. It creates greater internal congruence and integration in a person who is unusually disintegrated, by regulating their physiological stress response. Given that in doing so it regulates the overproduction of cortisol, self-injury probably protects against brain damage in people who have experienced, or are experiencing, long-term stress.

That self-injury can be shown to lower cortisol levels tells us that self-injury *does* indeed relieve stress, but, as cortisol production is a response to stress, and not a cause of stress, it does not tell us *how*. It has been suggested that self-injury may release the body's natural opiates, and it is interesting to note that heroin users often self-injure if they have no heroin. Other research shows that it seems to be the serotonin system rather than the opiate system that is related to self-injury. More research needs to be done in order for science to confirm exactly how people who self-injure are self-medicating. But, while we await confirmation, the idea that self-injury seems to work in this way can help us make sense of, and respect, what those who do it say about why they do it, and to understand and empathise much more deeply with their experience.

DISSOCIATION

Not everyone who injures him- or herself in order to regulate an internal state is regulating their stress response in the straightforward way described so far. Some people cope with their uncontrollable stress response by dissociating, and harm themselves in order to dissociate. Once dissociated from their body, these people usually become unaware of the pain of the injury as well as the intensity of feeling that they were seeking to dissociate from. Paradoxically, other people self-harm in order to end a period of dissociation, using the pain and physicality of injuring themselves to bring their awareness back to their body.

Most counsellors and therapists are aware of dissociation that is related to trauma, but may be unaware that many people also dissociate as a way of coping with the kind of uncontrollable stress response I described earlier. Dissociation as a means of coping with over-arousal may start in very early childhood as the distressed child who has given up screaming becomes psychologically withdrawn, 'blank' or 'floppy'. Schore (2003b) describes how the process of dissociating in order to cope with an overactivated stress response gets 'hard-wired' into the limbic system, resulting in an automatic progression in later life from over-arousal to dissociation.

Schore is specifically interested in the right-brain 'primitive' feeling states like shame, disgust, elation, excitement, terror, rage, and hopeless despair that the client was not helped to tolerate and recover from as a pre-verbal infant, and which remain unrecognised, unsymbolised and unintegrated in the adult client. He is also interested in the strategies the infant used to deal with being overwhelmed by these feeling states—i.e. dissociation and projective identification—and in how the feeling states and strategies become, in Gendlin's words, 'frozen whole' (Gendlin, 1970), ready to defrost instantaneously as a rupture occurs in the therapeutic relationship.

Schore sees the exploration and repair of ruptures in the relationship as an opportunity to bring the client's non-conscious feeling states into awareness, and for client and therapist to work together in making them tolerable. Experience that happens before language centres in the brain develop does not later become available to language, and so projective identification—the therapist feeling what the client feels—enables the client to communicate what she/he cannot say.

Schore proposes that projective identification, which is often described as working by mysterious means, actually occurs via a process of high-speed empathy in which the therapist generates a feeling state within themselves that simulates how she/he would feel if making the facial cues the client is making. We process facial cues incredibly quickly—in less than 30 milliseconds—and so this process happens well below conscious awareness, as does the process by which the client recognises that the therapist also feels what they feel, and seems to be able to tolerate doing so.

Schore emphasises the importance of not rushing this stage of mutual recognition, as it is vital in enabling the client to develop tolerance, acceptance and integration of their previously dissociated feelings. He conceptualises this process—which relies so heavily on the right-brain ability of the therapist to process fleeting visual information—as the therapist's right brain healing the client's right brain; and it eventually results, he claims, in the client developing a right-brain system than can regulate the intensity, frequency and duration of feelings more effectively.

Left-brain activity, specifically that of symbolisation—describing the body-mind feeling states in words and attributing meaning to them—is also important in helping the client develop the ability to reflect on the meaning and significance of feelings, as well as to express them in a more socially appropriate manner. Work with this client group involves both the right- and left-brain activity of the helper, which is why I have invited you to imagine what it might be like to be the baby or client I am describing. Visualising a right-brain activity—a flushed and screaming baby—and imagining what you might be feeling if you were that baby, is a similar process to the one Schore uses to describe the process of projective identification, and hopefully has evoked in you a bodily echo of what it is like to experience stress over which you have no control.

ISSUES FOR PRACTICE—PRESENCE AND PACING

Schore focuses on empathic attunement in working with clients who have been separated from their parent, neglected, or abused in infancy. My own experience leads me to give equal emphasis to the therapist's quality of presence. People who were treated violently, roughly, coldly or with indifference as children have often learnt to be very sensitive to the quality of another person's presence, and feel very easily invaded or abandoned. If the counsellor's presence is not very, very gentle, such a client is likely to feel threatened, and to remain stressed even after the perceived threat has passed.

Yet such clients need a very solid presence. The gentleness must not be psychological absence in disguise. The counsellor must be solidly and warmly there in a very gentle way. Being engaged and relaxed, rather than engaged and focused, is probably a good general guide to being solidly there in a gentle way. Of course, no general guidelines suit all individuals—the important thing is that the therapist is aware that the quality of their presence is likely to have a particularly strong impact on clients who self-injure in order to calm themselves, and that this can be reflected on in sessions and in supervision.

I recently got the quality of my presence wrong for a client of mine called Kia. I had overrun with the previous client, who had been doing some very deep work. Normally I potter around for a quarter of an hour between sessions, and this enables me to return to 'neutral' before I see the next person, but, on this occasion, I didn't have time to potter. I was not perturbed by my lack of a break, as I still felt energised and focused. I was, however, far too energised and focused for Kia. I sat down, leant forward slightly, focused my attention on her and waited for her to begin. She found this much, much too intense. She felt pressurised to say something by my expectant posture, and invaded by my eagerness to engage. Fortunately, our relationship was such that she was able to tell me, and I relaxed and backed off.

It is important that we hold the client's process just as gently, and are relaxed about the pace of work. Clients whose psychological and biological processes are out of synch spend much of their energy struggling to establish some inner equilibrium, and really do need to go at their own pace. It may take time for them to connect to how they feel, and once connected, they may need to tread very carefully to avoid becoming over-aroused and overwhelmed.

Kia says that the only thing that calms her down is chatting with me. She becomes very easily overwhelmed by her feelings, and focusing on them for too long can leave her hyper-aroused for days. She needs to pace herself very carefully indeed in order to avoid going into a state in which she wants to harm herself. But the chat is not simply avoidance. Sitting together and talking about something non-stirring and inconsequential enables Kia to use my embodied presence to help calm her physiological stress.

Chatting at length with clients is something that is generally frowned upon, and it is certainly important that if we are working with a client, we are working therapeutically, and not just lapsing into something that is essentially not much different from social contact. The client should be getting something they could not get from a social relationship. If I found myself chatting with another client, I might wonder if we were avoiding something; if we might be having problems recognising that the therapy was over, or if I was neglecting the boundaries of the therapeutic relationship in some other way.

Chatting is close to the boundary between therapy and friendship. It is my responsibility, as the therapist, to make sure that our relationship remains that of client/counsellor. My chats with Kia are always about her, or something neutral like a television programme. I am 'me' when we chat—I have opinions on the TV programmes etc.—but our chats are not *about* me. Kia is my client, not my friend. And she needs me to be her therapist, not her friend.

Whatever Kia and I may be chatting about, I believe our bodies are getting on with important work—her breathing becomes slower and steadier to match mine, and her heart rate slows so as to be in synch with mine. Not only does my body enable her body to calm down in the moment, but, hopefully, this kind of contact will, over time, help to change Kia's biological stress response, bringing it into a closer relationship with her psychological response.

If Kia has become stressed by her contact with me, and is keeping me at a psychological and physical distance, it becomes very important to her to be able to hold one of my cats. I have several cats, and Kia is fond of all of them, but if she needs to soothe herself, she chooses a particularly languid cat, who is habitually relaxed to a degree that is uncommon in man or beast, and who seeks psychological contact through leaning her relaxed body into Kia's, and gazing at her. In other words, my cat does what Kia's mother presumably did not. She uses her physical presence to make psychological contact, and to soothe, when words are not possible. My cat may well be helping Kia change her biochemical stress response by soothing her in such an embodied way.

When she is not keeping me at a distance, Kia sometimes asks me to soothe her in an active way: for instance, to stroke her head or hold her hand. However, therapeutic touch is an infinitely trickier business for me, or you, than it is for the cat. People who have been treated violently, roughly or coldly as babies, or whose parents did not respond to the 'I've had enough now—I need some space' signals that babies give, often feel invaded very easily as adults. Sometimes this is because they became so used to their boundaries being invaded that they have lost all sense of what does or does not feel comfortable. Sometimes it is because they are very wary of other people, and can easily experience contact as threatening, or just too 'full on'. Sometimes it is because they don't give themselves permission to say, or even be aware, that the contact feels too close. Often it is for all of these reasons.

I am not talking about sexualised contact, or even contact that the client misinterprets as sexualised. Peter Rutter's *Sex in the Forbidden Zone* (1990) is an excellent exploration of why sexual contact between therapists and clients is damaging to the client, and why so many therapists do it, or are tempted to. I am talking about touch that feels uncomfortable because it is just not what the client wants. Although this may sound innocuous compared to sexualised contact, it, too, is damaging.

Feeling that we have choice and control over how close other people come, or who touches us, and how, is vital to our basic sense of safety in the world. People who have had experience of hostile or unwelcome contact, especially as children, often do not have this basic sense of safety, and feel invaded and threatened very easily indeed. Because the experience of feeling invaded involves a sense of choice being taken away, of disempowerment and often of helplessness, it becomes even harder for the client to say that they want the therapist to stop.

I make sure that Kia asks for any physical contact we have, including how close she wants me to sit that particular day, and that she is specific about stroking her head or putting my hand on her shoulder, for instance. I have, on a few occasions, found myself putting my hand on her arm in a spontaneous gesture of comfort, but have noticed that I do so in slow motion, checking with Kia as I do, whether it is okay or not. I would pull back if I got anything less than a positive affirmation—no reaction is not necessarily permission.

Touch is a complete 'no-no' for many therapists because it is so risky. It is certainly not something to do if you feel uncomfortable or anxious about doing it, as this will be communicated in the quality of your touch, and defeat the purpose. It is wise, if you do touch clients, to make sure that there is a *continuous* dialogue going on about what is, or isn't, comfortable.

For many clients simply being in another person's warm and relaxed presence is sufficient physical contact. I find that the clients who have been abused or neglected the most severely and who self-harm the most seriously find it enough (and any more would be too much) to just sit with me in silence, slowly getting used to being within another person's presence without fear. Some clients need to do this for many sessions, or large portions of many sessions, before they are ready to do anything else.

ABSENCE

The quality of a therapist's absence is as important as the quality of their presence, particularly for clients who self-harm in order to reduce stress, and are using therapy to establish a sense of safety-in-relationship. It is a big, big deal for Kia if I take a holiday, or am unable to see her for some other reason. Sometimes we keep in contact by phone, particularly if she is in crisis. If I am ill, or having a complete break from work, she arranges to see someone else.

Whether we keep in touch by phone or she sees someone else, it is really important for her that she expresses how she feels about me going, and how angry she is with me for having gone. We both know that the more adult part of her understands perfectly well that if I am sick, I can't see her, and that obviously I need to take regular breaks from work; but the part of her that feels abandoned and frightened, the part that sends her physiological stress response into overdrive, and makes her want to cut herself, needs to be fully heard, understood, and accepted by me, even when she is incandescently furious with me for doing something perfectly reasonable.

Although I have written the last couple of paragraphs in the present tense, I am aware, and have become more acutely aware in writing it, that much of what I have described is no longer the case. It has been a long time since Kia has been incandescently furious with me for going on holiday, and she often says that she has felt soothed just by leaving a message on my answering machine. Whereas she originally kept contact with me by phone *and* saw someone else while I was away (and was furious when I got back), she now no longer sees someone else unless I am away for an unusually long period.

This movement towards needing my (or another therapist's) actual physical presence less has been a very important piece of developmental work for Kia. Because she was not sufficiently soothed by her mother as a child, but was subjected to verbal violence, she did not develop much ability to trust other people. Not only has Kia managed to develop trust in me, but she has also moved through a period of high dependence to a place from which a more abstract idea that I am there is almost as soothing as my actual physical presence. She knows that I am 'there', even when I am not in the same room, or even the same country.

Like a child who progresses from becoming distressed because its parent leaves to knowing that its parent will come back, Kia has learnt that I have not abandoned her by leaving, and that my temporary absence is tolerable. Whereas Kia would, in the past, cut herself a great deal if I was unable to see her, she now only cuts occasionally. She is, very slowly, becoming more able to regulate her own stress response without self-harming.

CONCLUSION

Research shows that self-injury reduces physiological stress, whether or not that particular person cites stress reduction as the reason for their self-harm. It also shows that there is a time lag between physiological stress being lowered, and the person who is self-harming actually feeling better. Both these discoveries suggest that many people who self-harm are regulating their internal state, but may be unaware that they are doing so. It is worth keeping this possibility in mind when working with someone who gives other reasons for hurting themselves. Many people self-harm for a number of reasons, some of which they may be aware of, some not.

It is important that we take particular care in working with clients who self-harm in order to regulate overwhelming stress or a dissociated state. Research into emotional and neurological development shows that a deficiency of love, attention, acceptance and empathy during certain windows of growth affects our future ability to regulate our feelings. It seems likely that a great many people who self-harm have suffered neglect resulting in a physiological stress response that is easily triggered, but not easily regulated. Work with these clients needs to be slow and careful if it is to be helpful rather than overstimulating.

REFERENCES

Caldjic, C, Diorio, J & Meaney, M (2000) Variations in maternal care in infancy regulate the development of stress reactivity. *Biological Psychiatry, 48*: 1164–74.

Chambers, RA, Bremmer, J, Moghaddam, B, Southwick, S,Charney, D & Krystal, J (1999) Glutamate and PDST. *Seminars in Clinical Neuropsychiatry,* 4(4): 274–81.

Collins, P & Depue, R (1992) A neural behavioural systems' approach to developmental psychology implications for disorders of affect. In D Ciccetti & S Toth (eds) *Rochester Symposium on Developmental Psychopathology, vol 4*. Rochester: University of Rochester Press.

Gendlin, ET (1970) A theory of personality change. In J Hart & TH Tomlinson (eds) *New Directions in Client-Centred Therapy* (pp. 129–73). Boston: Houghton Mifflin.

Gendlin, ET (1986) *Let Your Body Interpret Your Dreams*. Wilmette, IL: Chiron.

Gunnar, M & Donzella, B (2002) Social regulation of the cortisol levels in early human development. *Psychoneuroendocrinology, 27*: 199–220.

Haines, J, Williams, CL, Brain, KL & Wilson, GV (1995) The psychophysiology of self-mutilation. *Journal of Abnormal Psychology, 104* (3): 471–89.

Konyescsni, W & Rogeness, G (1998) The effects of early social relationships on neurotransmitter development and the vulnerability to affective disorders. *Seminars in Clinical Neuropsychiatry, 3*(4): 285–301.

Linehan, MM (1993) *Cognitive-Behavioral Treatment of Borderline Personality Disorder*. New York: Guilford Press.

Lyons, D, Lopez, J, Yang, C & Schatzberg, A (2000) Stress level cortisol treatment impairs inhibitory control of behaviour in monkeys. *Journal of Neuroscience, 20* (20).

McEwen, B. (1999)Lifelong effects of hormones on brain development. In L Schmidt & J Shulkin (eds) *Extreme Fear, Shyness and Social Phobia*. Oxford: Oxford University Press.

Rogers, CR (1951) *Client-Centered Therapy: Its current practice, implications, and theory.* Boston: Houghton Mifflin.

Rutter, P (1990) *Sex in the Forbidden Zone*. London: Unwin Hyman.

Sachsse, U, von der Heyde, S & Huether, G (2002) Stress regulation and self-mutilation. *American Journal of Psychiatry, 159*(4), 672.

Schore, AN (1994) *Affect Regulation and the Origin of the Self: The neurobiology of emotional development*. Hillsdale, NJ: Erlbaum.

Schore, AN (2003a) *Affect Regulation and Disorders of the Self*. New York: Norton.

Schore, AN (2003b) *Affect Regulation and the Repair of the Self*. New York: Norton.

Van der Kolk, B, Perry, C, & Herman, J (1991) Childhood origins of self-destructive behavior. *American Journal of Psychiatry, 148*(12): 1665–71.

Yehuda, R (1999) Linkingthe neuroendocrinology of post-traumatic stress disorder with recent neuroanatomic findings. *Seminars in Clinical Neuropsychiatry, 4*: 256–65.

Chapter 6

WHOSE FEAR IS IT ANYWAY? WORKING WITH YOUNG PEOPLE WHO DISSOCIATE

Theres Fickl

Some young people's routine response to fear is to dissociate. My aim in this chapter is to explore what follows from this process of dissociation, specifically for those young people who also self-harm. Although self-harm and dissociation are not always linked, dissociation does present particular issues for young people who also self-harm. Young people who have learnt to dissociate in order to survive are especially vulnerable in our services, because their self-harm is often misinterpreted and their dissociation largely ignored. A consequence of this is that self-harm and dissociation generate considerable fear and anxiety for people in the helping professions.

Fear is a protective mechanism as well as a great motivator to either dissociate or take control (Rowe, 1987). This chapter represents my search for ways of being in therapeutic relationships with young people, which are not based on fear. My aim is to demonstrate that people in the helping professions need to be aware of both their clients' and their own responses to fear. Both are crucial if practitioners are to be able to give and get support, and hence stay grounded, whilst engaging with these young people. As such, in thinking through these issues I also draw on my own experiences of personal therapy and supervision, where I have explored my own processes of dissociation.

I begin by defining the process and development of dissociation. I then use examples of my own and young people's experiences to illustrate the process of dissociation, and the ways in which dissociation links with self-harm. I explore the implications for practice by reflecting on my work with young people who dissociate whilst self-harming. Finally, I address the importance of supervision in validating and mapping feelings of fear, anxiety and the need for control, which may be experienced when working with this specific client group.

UNDERSTANDING DISSOCIATION

The process of dissociation can be seen on a continuum, ranging from being 'associated', to temporarily 'switching off', to 'blanking out', to 'cutting off' from the body, to 'splitting off' from parts of oneself, to developing an alternative self or alternative selves. Dissociation is a trauma-based condition, and is a way of surviving real life negative events. It is, as Sinason (2002: 4) argues, 'a brilliant piece of creative resilience, which comes with a terrible price'. Real life events might range from prolonged hospitalisation with continuous medical invasion of the body to having very insecure attachments with unpredictable caregivers, to severe and sadistic childhood abuse. As such, dissociation happens because:

> [W]hen children cannot physically get away from abuse, they must find ways of psychologically splitting off from the abuse instead. (Warner, 2000: 56)

Repeated experiences of trauma can, therefore, lead to chronic and habitual splitting of this nature. Gerhardt (2004: 162) describes the way in which a 'fleeing inwards' occurs, for example, when the person dissociates from her feelings altogether to escape the impact of a situation. Over time the individual can lose access to what we refer to in everyday language as 'gut feelings' (Turp, 2003: 145). Physiologically, a 'low down' occurs, with decreased blood pressure and heart rate. This could be compared to how some animals 'play dead' when faced with another predatory animal (Gerhardt, 2004: 162). In some situations a 'false self' (Turp, 2003; Winnicott, 1960) may then develop in response to persistent splits between physical, feeling and thought functioning. The real core self is hidden (that is, protected) behind a façade, a mask.

Hence, in the face of overwhelming distress the individual unconsciously splits off parts of themselves they do not like or cannot cope with. The individual may subsequently feel that 'my body is not me. I am not really here'. For some children and young people who dissociate this may ultimately result in the development of alternative selves or, what is currently termed 'dissociative identity' (previously known as having 'multiple personalities'). As indicated, dissociated identity commonly develops in the presence of severe, sadistic and repeated child abuse. This abuse is often perpetrated by a number of adults/caregivers against mainly female children (and hence, why I refer to 'she' rather than 'he' throughout this chapter). This form of child abuse sometimes includes organised or ritualistic elements. And it frequently begins at a very early age when the personality is developing (see Coleman, 2002).

Children, in this context, develop dissociated responses by unconsciously refusing to emotionally conceive that their caregivers are also the people who are harming and hating them. This development is reinforced by the abuser's demands for secrecy and by the absence of protectors. Over time, and in the face of repeated trauma, a 'dissociated identity' can develop, whereby children and young people split off parts of themselves and establish alter selves, which they then further dissociate from. These alter selves, or states, might not communicate with each other or have any knowledge of each other. Hence, the development of an 'alternative' self facilitates the avoidance of thinking. Bentovim (2002: 26) has described this as 'the Self without memory'. Whilst this may be an effective survival mechanism, it does mean that it can be difficult for both clients and professionals to process the things that trouble them, precisely because they cannot recall them (Sinason, 2005).

For example, when I began the process of writing this chapter, I became overwhelmed by my own fears about writing and found myself unable to think about 'dissociation', as I dissociated from the writing task. As such, I mirrored something of what I was trying to write about. In order to illustrate the relationship between stress and dissociation I draw on Warner's (in press) adaptation of 'Yerkes-Dodson's Law' (Yerkes & Dodson 1908/2006) (see Figure 1).

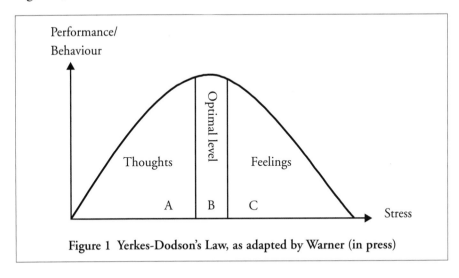

Figure 1 Yerkes-Dodson's Law, as adapted by Warner (in press)

According to Warner (in press: 357–8):

> In order to function in the world everyone needs a bit of 'stress' (or adrenaline) to get them going (without this we are asleep). However, if we get too stressed we stop being able to perform at all (point C). This is because we become overwhelmed by feelings. Nevertheless,

it is when we are (equally) connected with both our thoughts and feelings that we act at our optimal level (point B). Because it is hard to be connected with our feelings all the time most of us function (in therapy and other relationships) somewhere at about point A (that is mainly thinking, but in touch with our feelings).

In writing this chapter I have journeyed through all the points described above. I noticed that when I first sat down to write I was able to think clearly as I experienced only low to moderate stress levels (below point A). However, this rapidly gave way to chaotic and disconnected thought processes as I started to have an emotional response to what I intended to say (moving past point B and towards point C). As I became overwhelmed by my fears, my stress reached an intolerable level, and I was eventually unable to think at all (point C). At this point (point C) I dissociated. This had the effect of lowering my stress arousal. In this 'frozen' dissociated state I felt calm. However, I could not 'perform' and the deadline for writing the chapter loomed, which caused further fear and dissociation.

I could have remained stuck in this dissociated state and ultimately not have written this chapter. However, I enabled myself to re-access my thought processes by consciously using 'grounding' techniques (Zulueta, 2002). For example, using words and pictures I tried to reconnect with what I thought and felt, both physiologically and emotionally, in order to try to make sense of my frozenness, my dissociation. I wrote:

> My head feels empty and I feel frozen in my posture and trapped. I keep going to this safe place within my mind by just sitting and staring, suspending all thoughts, feelings and action. This allows me to be calm. I imagine that if I 'unfreeze' I will give in to the anxiety, which I can sense underneath. As I start breathing deeply and allow my anxiety to find words, I let myself know that my fears are about getting it wrong.

I resolved to talk to colleagues and supervisors about my worries of being found out as a 'bad professional', and reminded myself how helpful articles by professionals who 'self-disclosed' about their fears had been to me (see Wosket, 1999). Through writing, drawing, talking and reading I was able to process and contain my fears, such that I was able to sit down and write this chapter. Young people in our services may also benefit from similar grounding techniques. However, their dissociation may be more entrenched and far-reaching, and their need to stay dissociated more profound. As Zulueta (2002) argues, and the aforementioned example demonstrates, the process of dissociation can be a protective (rather than defensive) coping mechanism that enables the integrity of the self to be maintained in the face of both small and sometimes catastrophic trauma.

As indicated, dissociation 'works' as a coping strategy precisely because it prevents thinking, feeling or action about traumatic and/or abusive experiences. Young people may fear being 'found out'. This may be via their own discovery of the abuse, experienced by dissociated parts of themselves, and/or other people (such as professionals) discovering their secrets. Furthermore, fears of being misunderstood, labelled as 'mad and/or bad', disbelieved and dismissed, create an additional form of loneliness, which compounds the isolation that often conceals abuse. When feelings of shame, guilt and secrecy are connected with, further disconnectedness from others and alienation from the self might take place. These feelings are painful and frightening, and young people can further dissociate in response. Young people must then find ways to ground themselves after dissociation. One such grounding technique that these young people sometimes use to decrease the high emotional arousal that underlies dissociation (Figure 1, point C) is self-harm.

DISSOCIATING BEFORE, DURING AND AFTER SELF-HARM

As argued, the process of dissociation is a protective strategy that controls the effects of damage caused by overwhelming trauma. Self-harm further functions as a means through which people can gain a sense of taking and being in control (Spandler, 1996). Hence, control is an important aspect of both self-harm and dissociation. Most young people who self-harm are in control of their self-harm, inasmuch as they have awareness of the severity, and need for aftercare, of their injuries. However, when young people also dissociate, the control they would otherwise experience over, and through, their self-harm decreases *because* they are dissociated. The difficulty is that young people whose routine response to high emotional arousal is to dissociate are at greater risk of being out of control of their self-harming behaviour, precisely because they are also dissociated.

Young people who dissociate before, during or after they self-harm are not only at risk in terms of their physical survival; they are also vulnerable in terms of increased negative discrimination from professions. Their self-harm is even more distressing to professionals because it appears to be erratic and out of control. This is because the young person struggles to provide a clear and connected rationale for 'when', 'where' and 'how' her self-harm was triggered. Under such circumstances, it may be tempting for professional helpers to believe in the myth that self-harming behaviour is always and essentially attention-seeking behaviour, as this belief alleviates the professionals' own distress at not understanding the young person. Professionals may then turn to contracts or withhold services to try and control the self-harming behaviour. In order to be more supportive of these young people, professionals need greater understanding of what transpires when young people dissociate before, during and after self-harming. This is because the consequences for the young person are different depending on when dissociation occurs.

Young people who dissociate before they are aware of any intent to self-harm can later re-emerge from their dissociated state to discover their injury without being able to recall what occurred, nor knowing what triggered the self-harm. Triggers might include self-loathing, a flashback, an alter self taking over whose role it is to self-harm, or a general feeling of being overwhelmed by fear. Whatever the injuries and whatever the triggers, it is important to acknowledge that dissociation occurred before the person self-harmed. Hence, it is crucial that we listen to the language the young person uses to describe what they experienced. For example, when a young person says, 'I don't know how that happened!' we should not assume that she is avoiding taking responsibility for the self-harm. She may be actually indicating that she was not 'present' before the self-harm started.

A young person who dissociates whilst self-harming might injure herself to a far greater level of severity then they initially intended, and therefore needs to have access to services that will try to understand their dissociated state, rather then just address the obvious lack of control in their self-harm. The young person, herself, might be quite scared about the severity of her self-harm and need support in finding some understanding of the dissociated self-harm in order to regain some control in the future. A young person who dissociates after self-harming is less able to care for their physical well-being, and might only look for medical attention at a later stage, if at all. Irrespective of when self-harming young people dissociate, the risks involved in self-harm may be increased if they also perceive their living body as just a shell, which is numb and which they feel alienated from. As Goodwin (2002: 140) argues:

> [O]nly when a young person is convinced that the body self that remains is really her own living self, not just a mannequin, do ideas about self-care and safety have any meaning.

If we are to encourage these young people to care for themselves, then greater emphasis needs to be placed on the causes and effects of dissociation whilst training workers. Currently, the training of support workers and counsellors includes little teaching on the link between the development and processes of dissociation and self-harm. For example, my five-year training as a specialist residential support worker in Austria did not address 'grounding' techniques, self-care, supervision and self-supervision (this only happened when I trained as a counsellor). There were no discussions or explorations of our own coping strategies and our own dissociation in the face of fear when working with young people who self-harm and/or dissociate. In the residential homes there was an unspoken expectation that workers would just 'get on with it', the 'it' being our own feelings in relation to our work with young people. The message was to grow 'tougher'. We were actively encouraged to dismiss our feelings and dissociate from them and, with no appropriate place for me to take my feelings, I did just that.

My ability to dissociate protected me from my feelings of rage towards the perpetrators of abuse and from my sadness at the lack of protection young people (in the past and the present) had experienced. Yet, in my disconnection I did not know how to actively comfort these young people (nor myself), which left me feeling insecure, despairing and powerless. Their self-harming behaviour distressed me, and I felt helpless as I experienced difficulties in trusting young people to make good enough choices about their lives and their bodies. As my feelings overwhelmed me, I experienced fears of not being 'good enough' myself (Winnicott, 1960), of not being 'enough' at all (Rowe, 2004) and of yet again failing my clients. This further increased my need to dissociate; to 'do' rather than 'think or feel'; to control and manage not only the young people but also my own vulnerability (see Turp & Pointon, 2003). I needed help to understand and address my dissociation and need to control. This I found in books, training workshops, supervision and personal therapy. Like my clients, in order to change I needed support around understanding my process of dissociation. It did not help simply being told I was wrong when I rushed to control situations, just as clients are seldom helped by being told self-harm causes damage. Indeed, in therapy, it is far more important to help clients recognise why they dissociate, than to focus too much on the details of the 'what, when, where and how' of physical self-injury.

EXAMPLE FROM PRACTICE

To illustrate the implications for practice I am using the example of a young woman (who is a composite of different clients), who attends weekly counselling sessions. I include my own reflective thoughts about our work, which are written in italics. Her history is one of growing up in an environment of intergenerational abuse with no protection. She currently lives in supported housing, still has regular contact with her family, and engages in 'light' and 'severe' self-harm. She has accepted a label of 'attention seeker' because she cannot explain to herself why at times she finds herself having cut deeper than she initially intended. She describes herself as 'odd', 'numb' and 'not all there'.

I work with an integrative approach to counselling and have been influenced by the Gestalt approach of my own therapy. As argued, alter selves develop when children who suffered extreme experiences of neglect and intrusive abuse are not being protected. Subsequently silence, 'neutrality' and inconsistency in the helping relationship can be perceived as uncaring, detached, rejecting or abusive. In this sense 'adapting a warmer and more active and interrupting stance is more helpful' to the client (Sinason, 2002: 136). In the sessions, I attend to whatever the young woman brings for discussion each week, so that she controls what she wants to bring. I use the 'here and now' of our relationship to explore what is going on for her. As advised by the British Association for Counselling and Psychotherapy (2005: 6), when working with clients who self-harm I try to:

> ... ensure a good quality of care that is as respectful of the client's capacity for self-determination and their trust, as circumstances permit.

We negotiate some space for exploring the self-harm in terms of how she manages the aftercare and what might stop her from seeking medical treatment (on the occasions she needed it). I pay great attention to how she describes her experiences of finding herself with deep lacerations on her arm when she had initially only intended to make cuts on the first layer of skin to help alleviate her distress with 'flashbacks' to the abuse or after contact with her family.

> *I notice a sense of wanting to be in control and find it unsettling not to have any guarantee about the safety of her self-harming behaviour.*

I explain how dissociation can work as a protective process, and together we start exploring how she perceives herself before, during and after self-harming. We articulate what is happening for her internally (dissociation) and externally (self-harm). This enables the young woman to make a connection between becoming emotionally overwhelmed by her fears and/or feelings of powerlessness and suddenly finding herself with deep cuts to her left arm. I reflect back to her my awareness of when the young woman seems to dissociate in the sessions, for example when I experience her as 'absent', and by doing that start validating her experience. This allows her to acknowledge that she is neither 'odd' nor 'mad'.

For myself I acknowledge that I struggle when I feel 'shut out', because it feels familiar to me, and I know I can start feeling insignificant and both emotionally and physically 'not all there' myself.

Building up her awareness of when and how she dissociates increases her sense of control. Through this we explore her fear of, and frustration with, not feeling in control and look at ways of further taking back some control by exploring additional grounding techniques. Grounding techniques which particularly help include increasing awareness of the physical body. For example, she notes the chair she sits on, and how she holds onto the chair arms. She places her feet firmly on the ground as she tries to learn how to stay with her feelings without dissociating. This further increases her sense of control and allows her to start taking responsibility for herself and the management of her dissociated states. In the sessions I encourage her to try out what kind of physical and emotional distance she needs from me in order to feel safe and stay associated. Together we pay attention to the emergence of which thoughts, feelings and behaviours she is more likely to dissociate from.

I feel I keep losing my solid sense of self in relation to this young woman. I find myself wanting to extend the time boundaries just 'a little bit', to accommodate the young woman. I fear that anything less will be interpreted as 'I am letting her down', and a sense of 'I am losing her to the orbit of "numbness"'. At the same time I struggle and get fearful when she does not attend sessions, and I acknowledge that the hardest thing for me is to allow the young woman the space to come round to letting me care for her.

Together we identify different people who are available to her after the counselling sessions or when she thinks she might be especially vulnerable. These include friends and people from 'help-lines'. Additionally we explore how keeping a diary and dancing can support her with the process of connecting and disconnecting.

I note for myself the importance of not working in isolation with this young woman, for the isolation can fuel my own feelings of powerfulness and powerlessness.

Intrinsically, we are trying to integrate her past with her present, by working towards emotionally and cognitively taking on board what had happened in the past and how that has shaped her life today. The aim is to put together a coherent story of her life. I am open with the young woman about the fact that I use supervision for my own support, which allows her to know that she does not have to 'look after me'. She does not have to check out and assess how much of her pain and fear I can cope with. This is why supervision is so important when working with clients who dissociate and self-harm.

SUPERVISION

Supervision is a central form of support for professional helpers, where we can focus on our work and on how we are affected by it. We can reflect on our interventions and share some of our responsibility. As Hawkins and Shohet (1989: 20) argue:

> A good supervisor can help us to use our own resources better, manage our workload and challenge our inappropriate patterned ways of coping.

In the context of working with issues of fear and control, it is vital that external supervision (in addition to line management) is available in order to contain some of these powerful emotions. As professional helpers we need a space where we can reflect on how we think, feel and behave regarding young people's dissociation and self-harm, free of fear from repercussions on the integrity of our self and the security of our jobs. When I have only had line management supervision available to me in the past, this had consequences for my own professional and personal sense of self in as far as I developed signs of 'burn out' (Rothschild & Rand, 2006). Getting external supervision and further training made a huge difference to my ability to function effectively in my work.

At first I was distrustful of my supervisor. I feared she would not understand my clients and me, and needed a lot of reassurance about her expertise in the subject of working with young people who self-harm and dissociate. Hence, when I was encouraged to explore what was going on for me in relation to these young people, I 'froze' and 'numbed out' myself. In supervision the process of dissociation was named and acknowledged by both myself and my supervisor. I was supported to recognise how I mirrored the young people's dissociation. For example, what I feared most was that my lack of control would be perceived as 'bad practice' and a personal failure. Through supervision I was able to acknowledge that I had been locked into a 'parallel process' in the past (Wosket, 1999), as I dissociated alongside the young people in response to their, and my own, fears. I had worked in ways which left young people needing to resist my attempts to rescue them; defending against me as I persecuted, blamed and restrained them; or holding back and containing their own feelings in order not to 'upset' me.

This exploration supported me to face my fears and anxieties, and I felt contained by my supervisor, as these feelings emerged as meaningful. Hence, my emotional and physical responses to the process of dissociation and self-harm were validated and I stopped dismissing or dissociating from those feelings. As such, this allowed me to stay more present with the young person in the sessions without moving into control by rescuing, persecuting or rejecting them.

Supervision also allowed me to start putting together what I consciously and unconsciously observed during the course of a session with a young person, and it was that process of 'putting together the pieces' which helped me to gain a sense of control. I am supported in supervision to work through my distress in regard to the self-harm and my fears for the lives of these young people. I learnt to differentiate which clients, and which client material, would increase my feelings of fear and I would book in additional supervision accordingly. Supervision allows me to safely express my feelings, which have been elicited through the work, both within myself and through the client. This is important because the young person might not be able to share my concern for her, nor be able to share the expression of these feelings herself, due to her dissociation.

Goodwin (2002) highlights the importance of not working in isolation as professional helpers. This is because the lone support worker/counsellor might succumb to discouragement in the face of dissociation and self-harming behaviour and, as such, mirror the young person's feelings of loneliness, of no-being (Hobson, 1989) within the dissociated state. A supportive, containing and challenging supervisory relationship is vital for the well-being and continued functioning of the professional helper and can act as a reminder that she or he is not alone and unprotected, as the young person had been.

CONCLUSIONS

I have explored the link between dissociation and self-harm and demonstrated the role that control plays in both. By defining the process of dissociation in response to fear on both a personal and client level, I illustrated, on the one hand, the possibility of containment through grounding techniques and, on the other, the possibility of loss of control in self-harm. It is through developing an understanding of the process of dissociation that professional helpers are better equipped to support a young person in gaining some control over what is happening for them. Further, I argued that offering a consistent relationship, and long-term support to these young people is important for them to start making a difference in how they cope and live their lives. Making the process of dissociation visible opens up the possibility of working differently with young people who self-harm before, during or after dissociation. From this perspective the focus is on enabling young people to describe their experiences and supporting them in understanding their own process of dissociation, rather than concentrating on the injuries they cause to themselves.

In trying to answer the question of 'whose fear is it anyway?' I have drawn attention to how professionals sometimes mirror the same fear responses that clients demonstrate, and hence, why appropriate supervision and training is crucial for workers. Through support and validation of our own emotional and physical responses in supervision we might be able to role-model an 'associated self' in the sessions, no matter how dissociated and out of control we might feel at other times. Through the support of supervision I changed my ways of working, from wanting to control young people's behaviour, to engaging in therapeutic relationships that support young people to take more control of their own lives. It is, therefore, essential that I do the same. Ultimately, then, the aim is for both me and my clients to take control of our lives and feel less controlled by our fears and anxieties.

REFERENCES

British Association for Counselling and Psychotherapy (2005) *Ethical Framework for Good Practice in Counselling and Psychotherapy*. <www.bacp.co.uk/printable/ethical framework.html>.

Bentovim, A (2002) Dissociative Identity Disorder—A developmental perspective. In V Sinason (ed) *Attachment, Trauma and Multiplicity: Working with Dissociative Identity Disorder* (pp. 21–36). Hove: Brunner-Routledge.

Coleman, J (2002) Recognition of Dissociative Disorders. In V Sinason (ed) *Attachment, Trauma and Multiplicity: Working with Dissociative Identity Disorder* (pp. 197–201). Hove: Brunner-Routledge.

Gerhardt, S (2004) *Why Love Matters: How affection shapes a baby's brain*. London: Routledge.

Goodwin, J (2002) Snow White and the Seven Diagnoses. In V Sinason (ed) *Attachment, Trauma and Multiplicity: Working with Dissociative Identity Disorder* (pp. 139–48). Hove: Brunner-Routledge.

Hawkins, P & Shohet, R (1989) *Supervision in the Helping Professions*. Milton Keynes: Open University Press.

Hobson, RF (1989) *Forms of Feeling*. London: Routledge.

Rothschild, B & Rand, M (2006) *Help for the Helper: The psychophysiology of compassion fatigue and vicarious trauma. Self-care strategies for managing burnout and stress*. London: Norton.

Rowe, D (1987) *Beyond Fear*. London: Fontana/Collins.

Rowe, D (2004) *Women and Self-Harm workshop*, Leeds, November.

Sinason, V (ed) (2002) *Attachment, Trauma and Multiplicity: Working with Dissociative Identity Disorder*. Hove: Brunner-Routledge.

Sinason, V (2005) Dissociative Identity Disorder workshop, at the British Association for Counselling and Psychotherapy Conference, 2005.

Spandler, H (1996) *Who's Hurting Who?* Manchester: 42nd Street.

Turp, M (2003) *Hidden Self-Harm: Narratives from psychotherapy*. London: Jessica Kingsley Publishers.

Turp, M & Pointon, C (2003) Report: Self-harmers—a group apart? *Counselling and Psychotherapy Journal. 14* (5), 6–8.

Warner, S (2000) *Understanding Childhood Sexual Abuse: Making the tactics visible*. Gloucester: Handsell Publishing.

Warner, S (in press) *Understanding Women and Child Sexual Abuse: Feminist revolutions in theory, research and practice*. London: Psychology Press.

Winnicott, DW (1960) Ego distortion in terms of true and false self. In DW Winnicott *The Maturational Processes and the Facilitating Environment*. (pp. 140–52). London: Hogarth.

Wosket, V (1999) *The Therapeutic Use of Self*. London: Brunner-Routledge.

Yerkes, RM & Dodson, JD (1908/2006) *Yerkes-Dodson Law*. Accessed at <www.citadel.edu>, <www.upa.pdx.edu> and <www.csulb.edu/~tstevens/h71what.htm>.

Zulueta F de, (2002) Traumatic Stress and the Maudsley Hospital. In V Sinason (ed) *Attachment, Trauma and Multiplicity: Working with Dissociative Identity Disorder* (pp. 52–68). Hove: Brunner-Routledge.

Chapter 7

DISORDERED BOUNDARIES? A CRITIQUE OF 'BORDERLINE PERSONALITY DISORDER'

GILLIAN PROCTOR

In this chapter, I discuss the diagnosis of 'Borderline Personality Disorder' (BPD) and how it has been used to diagnose predominantly young women who self-injure and often who have survived abuse. 'Women at the Margins' is an activist group that is concerned about how the diagnosis of BPD pathologises and stigmatises women who struggle to survive experiences of abuse and oppression. The group put together a special edition of *Asylum* magazine on this issue which I co-edited (Shaw & Proctor, 2004). This chapter draws on some of the stories that women contributed to this issue. I discuss the implications of this diagnosis for young women who self-harm. I further discuss the reaction of mental health services to women given this diagnosis with particular reference to the notion of 'boundaries' and suggest that services often work to further stigmatise and take power away from young women. Instead I will suggest how mental health services could more usefully work to support young women and help them regain power over their own lives.

DIAGNOSIS

Like all psychiatric labels, BPD depends upon the practice of diagnosis. This practice, which is fundamental to psychiatry, is based on the assumption that mental illnesses exist in the same way that physical illnesses can be said to exist. It assumes that these 'diseases' can be identified and categorised as such by the mental health professional. This process is assumed to be scientific in the strictest sense of the word—based upon 'the accurate naming of an objective disease process' (Bracken & Thomas, 2000). Yet there is no physical test which can establish the presence of mental illness or disorder. Therefore diagnosis in mental health relies on the professional making observations and judgements about how a patient behaves, and about the thoughts and opinions she/he expresses.

Many psychiatrists suggest that mental 'illnesses' (such as 'depression' or 'schizophrenia') are caused by physical conditions such as chemical imbalances or faulty genes. Yet there is a large body of evidence and opinion which suggests that these 'illnesses' in fact result from experiences—the kind of lives we have had, the things that have happened to us, and the context of our lives now. Although people from both approaches produce evidence to support their beliefs—pointing to, for example, the prevalence of certain illnesses within one family; or to the large numbers of people in the mental health system who have had traumatic experiences—there is no absolute proof for either approach. Most of the evidence used to argue for biological causes could equally point to environmental causes, as nearly always, people who share genes also share environments (Joseph, 2003).

There is even more lack of clarity in psychiatry about the 'causes' of personality disorders. Mainstream organisations—such as Borderline UK (www.borderlineuk.co.uk)—suggest an amalgam of multiple approaches—that BPD may be the result of traumatic experiences and disordered thought processes, combined with a pre-existing genetic predisposition towards the disorder. This bio-psychosocial model is increasingly popular, yet often involves an emphasis on biological causes and treatments. With a body of confusingly competing ideas it is easy for authorities to pick on whatever suits whatever political aim they have at any given time. This is confirmed by a brief look at BPD-related sites on the Internet which overwhelmingly indicate that US-based research is focused on discovering physical causes for the disorder, and then finding medication to treat it.

WHAT DOES BPD MEAN AND WHERE DOES IT COME FROM?

The term 'borderline' was first used by analyst Adolf Stern in 1938 to describe patients who he believed were more disturbed than 'neurotic' patients but who, he believed, were not 'psychotic'. However, it was not until 1980 that BPD was first introduced as a diagnosable personality disorder in America. Now BPD is by far the most common PD diagnosis: one of ten personality disorders currently classified by the psychiatric classification system (DSM-IV). Self-injury is one of the primary diagnostic criteria of BPD. For a diagnosis of borderline personality disorder, five of the following 'symptoms' must be present (American Psychiatric Association, 1994).

- Unstable and impulsive
- Intense interpersonal relationships verging between idealisation and devaluation
- Affective instability and reactivity of mood

- Inappropriate intense anger
- Frantic efforts to avoid abandonment
- Identity disturbance; unstable self-image
- Suicidal and self-mutilating behaviours
- Chronic feelings of emptiness
- Transient stress-related paranoid ideas

SELF-INJURY AND BPD

However, research and my experience of working within the mental health system suggest that self-injury plays a much larger role in the diagnosis of BPD than this list would suggest. Herpetz et al. (1995), for example, demonstrate the importance of self-injury as a diagnostic criteria for BPD; whilst Habib (2001: 35) argues that BPD is 'the most common diagnosis given to primarily female self-harmers'. Indeed, it may often seem the case that simply being a woman who self-injures is enough to attract a diagnosis of BPD. Walker (2004: 21) illustrates this process:

> I was given the BPD label by a psychiatrist the first time I saw her. She started by asking me all the standard questions from her sheet until she had established there were times when I had harmed myself, at this point she only asked me questions which related to the diagnosis of BPD. I don't believe I would have been given this label if it weren't for my self-injury.

Often diagnoses are not made on the basis of long-term observations and relationships. Indeed 'research suggests that decisions made about patients are usually done so within thirty seconds to three minutes of the first contact' (Habib, 2001: 40). Suzi (2004: 12) recalls 'I saw doctors on the acute ward perhaps four times, so do not believe there is any way they had enough experience of me to draw any conclusions about the state of my personality'. When diagnosis is made so quickly, practitioners will rely on judgements based on what they perceive as obvious outward symptoms of mental illness or disorder. Self-injury may function as an easily, speedily identifiable symptom of BPD. Self-injury is not only visible and external, it is also a highly stigmatised act which challenges many of society's most deep-seated assumptions about how people ought to behave. It is a visible rejection of many of society's expectations of how women, in particular, should act and appear:

> Women are stereotypically caring, passive and image conscious. If you injure yourself you are not being caring towards yourself, self-harm can be seen as an aggressive act (although directed at yourself) and self-harm also seems to be in conflict with the stereotype of women being really image conscious. (Walker, 2004: 21)

Diagnosing behaviour as 'abnormal' and 'inappropriate' involves comparison to social norms and ideals; ways of behaving that the majority of people in a given society view as normal and acceptable. Given that self-injury is subject to so many negative associations and assumptions, it is likely to attract both the attention and the judgements of mental health professionals seeking to make a diagnosis. Stigma and judgement associated with people who self-injure are similarly associated with people given a diagnosis of BPD. Both are often assumed to be manipulative, attention-seeking, treatment-resistant, hostile and bring about feelings of anger, dismay and powerlessness amongst staff. It may well be that the major role that self-injury plays in the diagnosing of BPD has less to do with the objective scientific observation of diagnostic criteria than with the subjective judgements and feelings of mental health professionals. These judgements are often based upon socially shaped expectations of what is normal and acceptable behaviour—norms which are frequently constructed around gender.

IMPLICATIONS OF BEING DIAGNOSED WITH BPD

To be diagnosed with BPD can be a deeply stigmatising experience. Although there is no precise agreement on the meaning of 'personality', the lay consensus is that it in some way refers to the deeply personal essence of who we are. To say that the essence of who we are is 'disordered' is the ultimate invalidation of our humanity. 'To say that someone's personality is disordered or faulty is to place a judgement on someone's whole sense of "being"' (Walker, 2004: 21). This has particular resonance for people who have been abused: 'I spent much of my childhood being told directly and indirectly that I was mad, bad and that being treated badly was in some way my fault' (Suzi, 2004: 13). Women who, through experiences of abuse and trauma, were given the message that something is 'wrong' with them, are again marked out as disordered and blamed:

> Children are often made to feel responsible for the abuse that happens to them and made to feel that their emotions and responses to this abuse are inappropriate. Many survivors already have strong

feelings of blame and guilt for things they were not responsible for and had no control over: to label them as having BPD only reinforces these negative feelings. (Walker, 2004: 22)

It can be argued that diagnosis at least has a purpose if it leads to useful treatment. So what help have people with BPD been offered in mental health services? BPD has long been a diagnosis of exclusion from mainstream mental health services. Women are marginalised and stigmatised within services by being described as 'manipulative', 'untreatable' and 'attention-seeking nuisances'. It can be argued that, in practice, 'Personality Disorder' (PD) in general, is little more than a catch-all label applied to 'difficult' and 'non-compliant' patients: 'Personality Disorder appears to be an enduring pejorative judgement, rather than a clinical diagnosis' (Lewis & Appleby, 1988: 8). Further, 'in British mental health services it is very common for PD to be anything that cannot be accounted for in a patient by mental illness. PD is a dustbin category of problematic 'behaviour' as judged by significant others or staff' (Pilgrim, 2001: 255).

So what models of treatment are associated with this diagnosis? Historically, very few. In the minds of many who work within and use mental health services, the diagnosis of BPD carried an assumption of 'untreatability' the only hope being that you may 'grow out of it'; or that you may develop a 'more stable' personality disorder. Some people are offered dialectical behavioural therapy (DBT). The theory behind DBT suggests that women with BPD are unable to tolerate and 'regulate' their 'extreme' emotions. DBT focuses on teaching people diagnosed with BPD 'coping skills' to 'regulate their emotions'. The focus is on the present, as opposed to past experiences of trauma and on teaching people to think and behave in the 'right' ways, in particular to stop self-injury. Indeed, in DBT women are punished when they self-injure, inasmuch as they are denied contact with their therapist after self-injury (so as not to reinforce their behaviour). DBT is the therapy currently most publicised and seemingly popular with workers, being presented as the 'benign' response to BPD, as at least a service is offered. However, DBT carries an assumption that women with BPD are damaged creatures who need to be saved by the professional and taught how to be more 'appropriate'. It fails to address the personal legacies of abuse, and distracts attention from the endemic abuse of women and girls within this society. DBT has been renamed 'Diabolical Behavioural/Doing Bollocks Therapy' by survivor activist Louise Pembroke (who writes in Chapter 11 of this book).

BPD is a highly stigmatised diagnosis, with significant negative consequences both inside and outside of mental health services. Women already marginalised by society are further stigmatised by BPD, compounding feelings of guilt and shame. Some are already institutionalised and abused by mental health and criminal 'justice' systems, or have experienced unemployment, poverty and homelessness. Women are often lesbians, lone mothers, and other women who, in different ways, are considered to have 'failed' to live up to cultural, moral and normative expectations of what it is to be a woman in this society. Then, as a result of the BPD diagnosis, women are marginalised in society, for example by having their children removed, and are often unable to claim disability benefits but are too distressed and stigmatised to work:

> As they were dragged out, my eldest son was screaming for his comfort cushion. But I was already handcuffed and couldn't do a thing about these people taking my lovely children. I was sectioned and once again silent without a voice—the label had followed me in every walk of life. (Hurt, 2004: 23)

Women given the diagnosis of BPD can be further punished and blamed for 'needing too much' or 'resisting help', or sutured without anaesthetic in A&E. Can this diagnosis possibly be the start of a helpful service response to women in distress? Lack of services for people diagnosed with BPD was acknowledged and addressed by the British Department of Health paper, 'Personality Disorder: No longer a diagnosis of exclusion' (NIMHE, 2003) which suggests that mental health services need to be created and extended to offer help to people who have a diagnosis of PD. In 2003–4, £6.4 million of government money was distributed to 11 non-forensic pilot projects nationally to create new services specifically for people given the diagnosis of PD. In 2006 this money will be redistributed to the National Health Service Primary Care Trusts for the purpose of establishing and continuing PD services nationwide. The 11 pilot projects vary in the services that they offer. However, all of the projects stipulate that people must have a diagnosis of PD in order to be able to access the service.

It seems, therefore, that the exclusion of people with a diagnosis of BPD is to be addressed by the creation of services which respond specifically to PD diagnoses. In order to access such support, distressed people will need to attract and accept a diagnosis of personality disorder. As PD-specific services become an increasing presence within mainstream mental health services, so we might expect personality disorder diagnoses—including BPD—to increase in prevalence. This may have some profoundly negative consequences for those subjected to the diagnosis. Furthermore, in detracting attention from the endemic abuse of women and girls, it has negative consequences for society as a whole.

GENDER AND BPD

That BPD is a gendered diagnosis is beyond question—at least 75 per cent of those given the diagnosis are female (APA, 1994). However, the gendering of the diagnosis extends beyond statistics. For decades, feminists have written about how society is constructed around financial, social, physical, legal and other inequalities between men and women, and how these inequalities are related to our understanding of madness in women (see for example, Chesler, 1972; Johnstone, 2000; Ussher, 1991). These relationships are reflected in the feminist argument that the diagnosis of BPD is located within gendered structures of power and processes of understanding. This can be understood simplistically in terms of a dual approach:

1. *Labelled mad*: Women are labelled 'mad' when they don't conform to society's norms. This approach argues that the concept of 'madness'—rather than describing disease entities—is an idea which has been created by society to exclude and stigmatise people who refuse to behave as society expects they should.

2. *Driven mad*: Women are driven mad by their lot in this society. This approach looks at how women cope with life in a society in which they are less likely than men to have access to money, status, power and other resources, and are more likely to experience sexual abuse and violence.

WOMEN AND GIRLS LABELLED MAD

BPD is only one of the most recent diagnoses which apply particularly to women. Szasz (1972), for example, traces the history of the concept of madness all the way back to 'witchcraft'. Women who threatened social norms in the Middle Ages weren't called mad; instead they were called 'witches,' who could then be isolated and punished. Later, as science, medicine and psychiatry took over the social control function of the Church, the concept of 'hysteria' arrived in the nineteenth century.

Hysteria occupies a central position in the history of women's madness. It was used to indicate behaviours which are disapproved of, and these days is still used as a put-down when women express emotions: indeed, it is often applied to women who self-injure and/or have a BPD diagnosis. Feminists suggest that the behaviours which were diagnosed as 'hysteria' were in fact women's responses to their powerlessness in Victorian society; a reaction to the expectation that women should be passive, and an attempt to establish an identity for themselves instead of living by someone else's rules all the time (Showalter, 1985). Instead, they were subjected to a diagnosis which positioned them as sick and disordered; and which paid no attention to the powerless and often abusive situations that they were trying to cope with. I argue that the diagnosis of BPD is the latest example of this historical tendency to explain away the strategies which some women use to survive oppression and abuse, by describing these strategies as symptoms of 'madness'.

Chesler (1972) talks about how women are in a 'double bind'—that we can be labelled 'mad' both for conforming to, and for failing to conform to, mainstream expectations of feminine passivity. In the case of BPD, the diagnosis can be applied to women who fail to live up to their gender role because they express anger and aggression, which is unacceptable for women in this society. Conversely, the diagnosis is also given to women who conform 'too strongly', by internalising anger, and expressing this through behaviour focused on self, such as self-injury. In addition, the diagnosis of BPD is focused on the idea of irrationality which has long been associated with the feminine stereotype. Women are associated with emotionality, feelings and subjectivity, whereas men are associated with rationality, order and objectivity (Showalter, 1985). Emotions—already defined as 'mad'—are located within the individual woman, rather than understood as a reaction to the social context of women in distress. The act of diagnosing BPD depends upon a psychiatrist judging whether emotions are appropriate and healthy, with reference to the norm of 'rationality'. This means that both anger and fear of abandonment can be—and frequently are—judged to be inappropriate, as opposed to being understandable in the context of a person's history of being violated or abandoned.

> One of the suggested 'symptoms' of BPD is inappropriate anger. I believe that fighting back is an appropriate response. (Suzi, 2004: 11)

DRIVEN MAD: THE SEXUAL ABUSE OF WOMEN AND GIRLS

It is not hard to imagine how the contexts of women's lives—the pressures and oppressions that women have to cope with—can actually cause the feelings and behaviours which lead to a diagnosis of BPD. To say that we live in a male-dominated society usually provokes a lot of reactions. People like to point out how much things have changed in the past few decades for women. Yet many things remain the same. Women still earn much less than men; are overwhelmingly found in low-paid, low-status work, are massively under-represented in structures of power; are still largely responsible for childcare and housework; are sexually objectified in the media; told how our lifestyles, bodies and appearances should match up to a feminine norm, and stigmatised and excluded if we 'fail'. Without a doubt, this has a huge impact on women's mental health.

One important feature of women's experience of society is the sexual abuse of women and girls. Research has shown that between one in ten and one in three women will have experienced sexual violence or abuse at some point in their lives (e.g. Women's Support Project, 1990). Research indicates that the figure for women with a diagnosis of BPD is even higher. The 'Women's Mental Health: Into the mainstream' document acknowledges that many women with a diagnosis of BPD have a history of trauma (Department of Health, 2002). Castillo (2000) found that 88 per cent of the people she talked to who had a diagnosis of BPD had experienced abuse. For 70 per cent of women diagnosed with BPD this was early sexual abuse—the highest prevalence of association between gender and diagnostic categories (ibid.). This is reflected in other research, as well as in my experience.

Much research supports the belief that self-injury often functions as a means of coping with the effects of sexual abuse (see, for example, Bass & Davis, 1988; Arnold, 1995; Walker, 2004). Fifty per cent of the women who took part in Lois Arnold's 1995 research 'Women and Self-Harm' disclosed sexual abuse as one of the causes of their self-injury, as well as physical and emotional abuse, neglect and other factors. Self-injury can function as a powerful coping strategy for surviving the sometimes overwhelming feelings and situations associated with abuse. Yet frequently the prevalence of child sexual abuse is misrecognised and underestimated.

THE FALSE MEMORY SYNDROME AGENDA

The history of societal responses to childhood sexual abuse is a history of denial and distortion (Shaw & Proctor, 2005). Freud presented women's stories of sexual abuse as memories of fantasies rather than actual experiences and as a result the extent and impact of childhood sexual abuse was hidden for nearly a century (see Masson, 1985). In the 1970s and 1980s, childhood sexual abuse began to regain some limited recognition as an important issue. Yet very quickly, it met with a similar response in the form of 'false memory syndrome': a term which was invented by the founders of the False Memory Syndrome Foundation in the USA in 1992 to refer to 'memories of sexual abuse they believe are not real and which have been planted by a therapist or which have been "borrowed" by the person hearing accounts of sexual abuse' (Follini, 1995: 12). This 'syndrome' rapidly gained a lot of media attention. This illustrates how, wherever there is any recognition of the extent and the impact of the sexual abuse of women and children, there then follows a backlash: an attempt to deny sexual abuse and to invalidate those who expose its prevalence and its impact (e.g. Hill, 2004).

BPD reinforces this 'false memory syndrome' agenda by distracting attention from how psychological distress is often rooted in the experience of childhood sexual abuse. The mental health implications of sexual abuse are well-substantiated, both in research and theory (e.g. Finkelhor, 1986) and in direct accounts. 'I had flashbacks, terrifying anxiety symptoms and felt so dirty that I could barely walk down the street' (Suzi, 2004: 11). The 'symptoms' defining BPD can often be better understood as attempts to cope with experiences of sexual abuse and other kinds of trauma.

Instead, when people are given a diagnosis of BPD, this context of abuse and trauma is obscured as an important factor in a women's distress. The focus is placed on her as an individual: defining her as defective and disordered, and failing to recognise her 'symptoms' as appropriate expressions of feeling, and as ways of coping and surviving. As a nurse consultant describes in Warner and Wilkins (2003: 173): 'it's then that this person is like this for some reason that we don't know'. The only explanation that is offered is the diagnosis. Why is this woman distressed and self-injuring? Because she has BPD. Why does she have BPD? Because she is distressed and self-injuring:

> Instead of recognising the devastation caused by rape and child sexual abuse, honouring and supporting a women's survival, she is described as in need of treatment or perhaps 'untreatable'. (Hill, 2004: 16)

POWERLESSNESS

I have argued previously that the experience of powerlessness is a significant causal factor in the experience of psychological distress and the causes of distress (Proctor, 2002a). Within the psychiatric system, a survivor of sexual abuse is subject to a profound loss of control over her own life, as power is assumed by the psychiatric professional, who, through diagnoses such as BPD, has the power to define a woman's distress, to make statements about her 'prognosis' and to determine what 'treatment' is available to her (Johnstone, 2000; Proctor, 2002a; Shaw, 2004). In short, psychiatric responses and even psychological therapies (see Proctor, 2002a) can actually worsen the impact of abuse by 'denying to victims the healing experience of informed consent. They reinforce her status as victim, ignore her capacity for survival, and undermine her recovery' (Koss & Harvey, 1991: 133). It is not surprising then that these systems often fail to help survivors and people labelled with

BPD, but then this can be further used to blame people for 'resisting' help. One of the key concepts arising from these systems of power and control is the concept of 'boundaries'.

DISORDERED BOUNDARIES?

One of the concepts most frequently mentioned in the philosophy and rationale for new PD services is the importance of boundaries. 'Boundaries' are usually explained as the importance for clients of the therapist or worker setting limits which are predictable and consistent. The idea originates in psychodynamic therapy, based on Freud and other psychoanalytic theorists. Clearly the notion that workers need to be aware of the vulnerability of clients and take care to not abuse or exploit clients in their relationship is paramount. But this focus on boundaries has other effects not as benign as avoiding exploitation. This model is of an expert therapist, who can interpret and predict a client's needs. Boundaries usually refer to the timing of sessions and to rules limiting contact between therapist and client outside the session time. Often a picture is painted of a client diagnosed with BPD 'pushing' the boundaries of a therapist or 'resisting' the therapist's boundaries, and the usual advice given to therapists is of the danger of 'giving in' to the client. Already we can see the links between this approach and the common stereotype of women diagnosed with BPD as 'manipulative'. Indeed, the 'symptoms' of BPD include reference to no boundaries in relationships. It seems that women with this diagnosis are seen as deficient in their ability to have 'boundaries' in relationships and so it is the worker's job to help them by setting boundaries for them.

This seems to be a response to the history of mental health services failing to offer a service that works for people who are often diagnosed as 'personality disordered'. When clients ask for help outside their allocated appointment times, or complain about the help they have been given, or communicate in other ways that the services offered are not enough, the result has historically been for services to blame the clients for this response and constrain their services even further. The discourse of 'boundaries' serves to blame the clients for the service not working. Often appointments are offered at specified times in advance, which will not serve a need for a client in crisis. When clients turn up to such services, because no crisis provision has been arranged, the clients are blamed, rather than a lack of care planning being identified. When clients do not 'get better' in a specified timescale, rather than blame the lack of long-term services, the client is blamed for being 'unable to use a focused intervention'. This then justifies women with the diagnosis being blamed when the boundaries set by the services mean that services are not offering enough to help when a woman is distressed. Consequently, the woman herself is labelled as being 'too needy' (e.g. see Proctor, 2002b). This message can reinforce how women may see themselves, as being unworthy of care, and can increase distress at times when women are most in crisis.

The standard 'professional' model of care can ignore the subjectivity or personhood of the therapist or worker. The danger here is that these ignored needs are projected onto the client and then used to justify the therapist's own limitations as being 'boundaries for the good of the client'. For example, a worker with many responsibilities becomes increasingly frustrated with a client who regularly turns up in distress wanting to speak only to this worker. The worker decides the client is 'overstepping boundaries' and introduces a rule that the client can only turn up once a week, explaining to the client that these boundaries are for her benefit. The worker does not explain that she is unable to keep up with all her responsibilities and has reached a limit. Instead, the ethics of mutuality lead to more equitable relationships based on mutuality, where each has needs and limitations and these are discussed openly and honestly (see Proctor, 2004: 24–5). This is preferable to relationships based on dominance and submission: the more usual model for relationships in our society (Benjamin, 1988).

A major difficulty in discussions of 'boundaries' is the danger of workers constraining themselves to avoid potential abuse, but totally missing the danger of neglect. Taylor (1990) suggests that most women have already experienced too much emotional remoteness and that relating to a real person in a helping relationship is an essential part of empowering women. This is even more likely to be the case when working with women who have histories of abuse and abandonment. A refusal to be authentic and present in relationships can be experienced as abusive, and can result in harm. Heyward (1993: 137) notes:

> It was becoming increasingly clear to me that abuse—damage, harm, violence—can result from a professional's refusal to be authentically present with those who seek help; and that such abuse can be triggered as surely by the drawing of boundaries too tightly as by a failure to draw them at all.

As mental health services are currently struggling with how to respond to recent government legislation suggesting that BPD should not be a diagnosis of exclusion from services, surely the bottom line of any service aims should be to avoid making women's and girls' distress worse. We, as service providers, should not constrain ourselves by arbitrary or theoretical boundaries that restrict our human capacity to respond to people and care. Why should our boundaries be constrained by anything more than our own limitations of comfort within which we can look after ourselves and be able to honestly and openly respond to the needs of women and girls in distress?

DEFENSIVE OR HEALING PRACTICE?

A far better way to deal with the inevitable limits to what services can offer would be for mental health workers to be honest about their own limits and express them as such without trying to pretend that these limits are good for the client. If workers could be more honest about their limitations, then clients' need for other support and services could be identified and filled elsewhere. With this honest and mutual exchange, there could then be real attempts to fill the gaps in services and try to provide what women say they need.

To take the ethics of mutuality seriously is a big commitment, emotionally and politically. It requires clear commitment to our own self-awareness and a willingness to discuss the ethics of our decisions and ways of being with clients. If we want to take seriously the healing potential in mutuality, this will not be an easy or safe process. It has the potential to transform mental health services and indeed all our relationships. However, we cannot work this way without strong relational networks of support and solidarity.

CONCLUSION

In this chapter, I have taken a critical look at the growing prevalence of labelling women with BPD. BPD was presented as a particularly controversial diagnosis, which is highly stigmatised, with no agreed cause and few associated treatments—in practice, a catch-all label applied to 'difficult patients'. Many girls who self-injure are likely to end up being diagnosed with BPD, as self-injury is a highly stigmatised form of behaviour, which challenges many of society's norms and expectations. Women's and girls' distress can be understood as a response to our experiences in a society where power is shared unequally between men and women. Referring to a large body of feminist work, BPD is situated in a long history of responses to women's distress, denying the impact and extent of childhood sexual abuse. The diagnosis of BPD is criticised for focusing attention on the individual woman, rather than on the context of her life.

Women and girls who have been sexually abused or traumatised must have their needs and experiences taken seriously and feel a sense of control over treatment within services. Women and girls need people who respect the strengths and qualities that have helped them survive. Workers are needed who see women and girls as equals and as the experts on their own lives. Women and girls need to be understood in the context of our lives and relationships. We need mental health services to see sexual abuse as an issue that affects the whole of society, and which needs a political and societal response. Diagnosing women with borderline personality disorder achieves none of this.

ACKNOWLEDGEMENT

Gillian would like to acknowledge Clare Shaw for her contribution to this chapter. Parts of this chapter are taken from unpublished writings by Clare about borderline personality disorder: women, sexual abuse and self-injury.

REFERENCES

American Psychiatric Association (1994) *Diagnostic and Statistical Manual of Mental Disorders: fourth edition.* Washington DC: American Psychiatric Association.

Arnold, L (1995) *Women and Self-Injury: A survey of 76 Women* Bristol: Bristol Crisis Service for Women.

Bass, E & Davis, E (1988) *The Courage to Heal.* US: Vermillion.

Benjamin, J (1988) *The Bonds of Love: Psychoanalysis, feminism, and the problem of domination.* New York: Virago.

Boyle, M (1990) *Schizophrenia: A scientific delusion?* London, New York: Routledge.

Bracken, P & Thomas, P (2000) Postmodern diagnosis. *Openmind, 106:* (Nov/Dec), 19.

Castillo, H (2000) You don't know what it's like. *Mental Health Care, 4* (2), 42–3.

Chesler, P (1972) *Women and Madness.* Jovanich: Harcourt Brace.

Department of Health (2002) *Women's Mental Health: Into the mainstream. Strategic development of mental health care for women.*

Finkelhor, D (1986) (ed) *A Sourcebook on Child Sexual Abuse.* London: Sage.

Follini, B (1995) 'F.M.S.: Fraudulent, Misogynist and Sinister', *Trouble and Strife, 31,* 12–14.

Habib, A (2001) *Women, Self-Harm and BPD.* Unpublished dissertatation, John Moore's University, Liverpool.

Herpetz S (1995) Self-injurious behaviour: Psychopathological and nosological characteristics in subtypes of self-injurers. *Acta Psychiatr Scand, 91,* 57–68.

Heyward, C (1993) *When Boundaries Betray Us: Beyond illusions of what is ethical in therapy and life.* New York: HarperCollins.

Hill, M (2004) Breaking the Silence around Sexual Violence. *Asylum—The Magazine for Democratic Psychiatry 14*, (3), 16–17.

Hurt, S (2004) Sylvia Hurts. *Asylum: The magazine for democratic psychiatry, 14* (3), 23.

Johnstone, L (2000) *Users and Abusers of Psychiatry*. London: Routledge.

Joseph, J (2003) *The Gene Illusion: Genetic research in psychiatry and psychology under the microscope*. Ross-on-Wye: PCCS Books.

Koss, M & Harvey, M (1991) *The Rape Victim—Clinical and community intervention*. London: Sage.

Lewis, G & Appleby, L (1988) Personality Disorder: The patients psychiatrists dislike. *British Journal of Psychiatry 153*, 44–9.

Masson, J (1985) *The Assault on Truth: Freud's suppression of the seduction theory*. UK: Penguin.

NIMHE (2003) *Personality Disorder: No longer a diagnosis of exclusion*.

Pilgrim, D (2001) Disordered personalities and disordered concepts. *Journal of Mental Health (2201) 10* (3), 253–65.

Proctor, G (2002a) *The Dynamics of Power in Counselling and Psychotherapy: Ethics, politics and practice*. Ross-on-Wye: PCCS Books.

Proctor, G (2002b) My experience, as a client, of power in the therapy relationship. *The Journal of Critical Psychology, Counselling and Psychotherapy, 2* (3), 137–48.

Proctor, G (2004) Disordered boundaries. *Asylum: The magazine for democratic psychiatry, 14* (3), 24–25.

Shaw, C (2004) Sexual abuse: The psychiatric response and the construction of better alternatives. In G Proctor & MB Napier *Encountering Feminism: Intersections between feminism and the person-centred approach* (pp. 141–153). Ross-on-Wye: PCCS Books.

Shaw, C & Proctor, G (2004) Women at the Margins. *Asylum: The magazine for democratic psychiatry, 14* (3), 8–10.

Shaw, C & Proctor, G (2005) Women at the margins: A critique of borderline personality disorder. *International Journal of Feminism and Psychology, 4*, 483–90.

Showalter, E (1985) *The Female Malady: Women, madness and English culture, 1830–1890*. London: Virago.

'Suzi' (2004) Suzi's Story. *Asylum: The magazine for democratic psychiatry, 14* (3), 11–13.

Szasz, T (1972) *The Myth of Mental Illness*. London: Paladin.

Taylor, M (1990). Fantasy or reality? The problem with psychoanalytic interpretation in psychotherapy with women. In E Burman (ed) *Feminists in Psychological Practice* (pp. 104–18). London: Sage.

Ussher, J (1991) *Women's Madness: Misogyny or mental illness*. UK: Harvester Wheatsheaf.

Walker, T (2004) Why Cut up? *Asylum: The magazine for democratic psychiatry, 14* (3), 20–2.

Warner, S & Wilkins, T (2003) Diagnosing distress and reproducing disorder: Women, child sexual abuse and 'borderline personality disorder'. In P Reavey & S Warner (eds) *New Feminist Stories of Childhood Sexual Abuse* (pp. 167–86). London: Routledge.

Women's Support Project (1990) *Violence against Women Survey*. Glasgow: Women's Support Project.

Chapter 8

'TO THAT PIECE OF EACH OF US THAT REFUSES TO BE SILENT'[1] WORKING WITH SELF-HARM AND BLACK IDENTITY

VERA MARTINS

As a black practitioner and a manager I have been struck by the invisibility and silence around voices of black young people in much of what is written in the mainstream on self-harm. My experience in practice is that black young people also self-harm and I argue that much can be learnt from black identity-based work to inform more generic non-stigmatising work with other young people who self-harm. The aim of this chapter is to demonstrate how a focus on identity can inform work with black young people who self-harm and possibly have a relevance to more generic and non-stigmatising work with young people who self-harm. I will explore the interface between identity-based work and self-harm-focused work through theories of black identity and, in particular, the experiences of two black young people.

SELF-HARM, RACISM AND IDENTITY

Self-harm like racism and other structural oppressions is not a neutral subject. It is heavily loaded for a whole range of reasons—but predominantly because it is seen as the action of the 'other'. Self-harm is often what 'someone else does'. It is something 'out there' and the more physically 'graphic' and visible it is, the more evident and dominant become issues of control and containment.

There is still an overwhelming pressure to understand self-harm as part of the continuum to attempted suicide. The underlying message here is the powerful need to control and contain, perhaps in order to make 'us' comfortable and able to sleep at night. To describe self-harm purely in terms of extremes—risk to life and managing this risk—can have the effect of silencing those who self-harm, and who have a need to do this in a safe way.

1. Lorde, 1988: 5.

It often feels that the term 'self-harm' alone evokes panic, uncertainty and the need to 'cover up'. This then encourages silence and the need to make self-harm invisible in both a literal and symbolic sense. For many of the young people who self-harm, it is often quite simply about being alive, surviving in a hostile world, feeling and taking control of their bodies in a world that has silenced and sanitised who they are and their sense of self. Thus control and containment might in a very real way suffocate the emergence and nurturing of a sense of self and unique identity. Like issues of self-harm, issues of 'identity' also grapple with the concept of the 'other'. It can be argued that the more visible difference is, the more pressure there is to control and contain. This is particularly significant around issues of race and colour.

Since 9/11, the issue of racial identity and difference has taken on a whole new negative dimension. Difference, and being viewed as the 'other', is now inextricably linked with national security, and the response to the 'control and containment' of some communities has led to a greater visibility and assertion of difference. An example of this might be a young Muslim woman 'choosing' to wear the hijab or the burkha, thus making a powerful statement about her racial identity but at the same time possibly compromising her gender identity. It is these kinds of contradictions and conflicts that, when working with black identity, emphasise the importance to fully engage with the impact of racism (both institutional and individual) so as to inform our understanding of issues of identity and self-harm:

> A family do not leave their home after 7 in the evening; they stay in one large room, having barricaded their ground floor. A family are held prisoner in their own flat by a security cage bolted to their front door by white neighbours. A youth is slashed with a knife by an older white boy ... a family home is burnt out and a pregnant woman and her three children killed ... this is part of the black experience ... part of black people's reality. (Gordon, 1990: v)

Although this was written over 15 years ago, it can be argued that little has changed. With the murder of Stephen Lawrence, daily reports of attacks on taxi drivers and families, and the recent murder (2005) of Anthony Brown, a young African-Caribbean man from Liverpool, suggest that the harsh face of racial violence is still a reality for black people in the UK.

There is little doubt that the impact of violence and abuse on children from black minoritised communities is manifold. Their marginalised position in society and their representation in the mass media continually position them as the 'other'. This directly influences and gives an extra dimension to issues which are important to the lives of many black young people such as keeping secrets, family and community honour, racist backlash, identification with the abuser, guilt and shame. This may also be compounded by other experiences of oppression such as the homophobic bullying of lesbian and gay young people. It can also reflect the identity experiences of oppression of other minoritised and marginalised young people, for example, being a disabled young person. Such experiences of oppression can directly feed into and influence young people's negative sense of self and can contribute to high levels of self-harm.

As a practitioner, I have done considerable work with black young people around issues of self-esteem and identity. The framework I used was informed by the Cross and Parham model of black identity (Cross, 1971; Parham, 1989; Cross et al., 1991). It is the use of this framework with black young people that has led me to reflect on whether this kind of identity-based work could model a way of working with issues of self-harm in a non-stigmatising and developmental way. When working with issues of black identity, it is dangerous to ignore the place racism (institutional and individual) plays in polarising the behaviours and experiences around embracing identity. In a similar way, when working with young people around issues of self-harm, it is absolutely essential to acknowledge and engage with both the political and social context of self-harm.

THE CROSS AND PARHAM MODEL OF BLACK IDENTITY

The Cross and Parham Model of Black Identity Development identifies the crucial stages of black identity development through adolescence into adulthood. It suggests that the development of a black identity can be seen in five stages that are briefly summarised below:

1. *Pre-encounter stage* (Absorbtion): The individual absorbs and accepts white Eurocentric perspectives and sees him or herself in this way.

2. *Encounter stage* (Experiential): A particular experience or event shocks the young person sufficiently to see themselves differently in relation to race/racism. There is a tentative openness to explore new ways of seeing themselves and the rest of the world.

3. *Immersion-Emersion stage* (Reaction): The young person completely immerses themselves into her/his identity and what it means to be black. This is often a heightened emotional stage and can result in anger or even withdrawal.

4. *Internalisation stage* (Positivity): The individual is no longer inward looking or concerned with how others might see or define them, but is more confident and proud of their identity. They engage with wider struggles and will form alliances with groups of people where there is mutual understanding and respect.

5. *Internalisation-commitment stage* (Confidence): The individual achieves and embraces an understanding of the changing nature of their identity and is able to negotiate complex roles and responsibilities with critical awareness.

In the following sections I apply this understanding as a framework for understanding my work with two black young people who self-harm. Their names and some reference points have been changed to ensure anonymity. The quotations included are statements that they have given me permission to use.

UTIM

I met Utim whilst I was working in a refuge. Utim was born in the UK, is of Pakistani heritage and a Muslim. He was 11 years old when I started working with him. Utim often presented as withdrawn and I communicated with him through artwork. Using the above model, at the point of engaging with Utim, he appeared to be at the Pre-encounter stage (1) inasmuch as he would not acknowledge his Pakistani-Muslim identity.

At one of my early sessions I asked Utim to draw me a picture of how he saw himself. He insisted that I go and find white drawing paper as the coloured and cream paper would simply not do. I remember wondering whether this was about avoiding doing the drawing, but it was easy enough to find white paper. I gave Utim the paper. He then proceeded to draw and colour in with a dark brown pencil a big blob on the paper. I asked him to explain his drawing to me and he said that the 'blob' was himself. He went on to describe this as: 'a mega coffee stain on a white tablecloth'. I was stunned and silenced by the power of this image. It was necessary to further explore Utim's perception of himself as a 'blob' in order to have a better sense of where he was located in his identity journey.

The Cross and Parham model suggests that Utim may have been either in the *Encounter* (2) or *Immersion stage* (3). I went on to explore whether the 'blob' had to be a coffee stain or could it be a tea, milk or even a Ribena stain. He loved the idea of the Ribena stain but pointed out that he was not a 'Red Indian'. The 'milk' stain did not even apply. It would not show up on the tablecloth. As for the 'tea' stain, it could only apply if I was prepared to describe it as a 'chai' stain. I remember our discussion as if it were only yesterday. The imagery has stayed in my head and I will somehow always associate coffee with Utim. When I asked him why he preferred to be seen as a 'coffee stain' he said that it was because it was difficult to come out in the wash but it was possible to use bleach to make the stain fade away. This confirmed to me that Utim was at the *Encounter stage* (2) as he had obviously made connections about his difference. Although he was very angry and distressed, he was not at the *Immersion stage* (3) because he had not begun to completely immerse himself into his identity.

After extensive exploration of this symbolism it became clear that the event that had triggered this was something he overheard me saying to my co-worker. Most poignant was his remark 'I heard you talking about a film called *Coffee-Coloured Children* to Zaira and thought you were talking about me'. This could be seen as one of the events that made Utim think about himself in relation to racial difference in the world. I was curious and explored why he had thought I was talking about him to my colleague. In our discussion Utim talked about the difficulty of living in a refuge where he could not share the location with his friends. He felt he had to tell them that he lived with his Aunt. He also said that within the refuge, women talked openly to each other. He felt everyone knew everything about each other. He also talked about liking the fact that he looked like 'coffee' and remembered on one occasion describing himself as a 'toffee head'. Utim liked the relationship between 'toffee' and coffee' so hence the 'coffee stain'. However, his real struggle was around the expectations of the adults around him—his mother, his father, his teachers and to some extent myself. Over the next few weeks we spent time exploring expectations that adults had of him. We particularly focused on whether my expectations of him made our sessions difficult.

The focus of my work was to support Utim to move into the *Immersion/ Emersion stage* (3). Interestingly, he described my expectation of him as being one of pride, and he referred to one of the tunes I hummed to myself, which was 'being black and I am proud'. This could be seen as another Encounter incident. It was in our discussion around this where he took a big risk and talked very graphically about the colour of his skin and what it meant to him:

> It follows me everywhere ... in the classroom, in the playing field, on the bus ... it is there all the time ... and with it come the jibes and the jeers, the spittle and the shit ... and every night I scrub it and scrub it and scrub it ... and it won't go away.

It was at this point that I made real sense about the way he held his body— the slightly hunched shoulders—and why he kept getting into trouble at school. He either developed stomach pains before PE sessions or refused to wear anything other than long sleeves. It took me time to build a trusting relationship with Utim. He constantly tested me out and pushed quite hard for me to 'reject' him.

Our relationship was often turbulent, particularly because I struggled with the images of Utim scrubbing his skin raw. At times this impacted on my ability to really listen to what he was saying. I sometimes had an overwhelming urge to hold him and plead with him to stop hurting himself. I had to acknowledge my feelings but also had to learn to manage them so that Utim's 'space' was his and not mine.

Much of this work around building a trusting relationship moved between the *Encounter* (2) and *Immersion* (3) stages. It was necessary for Utim to immerse himself and learn to externalise his anger in a safe way. We worked at how he expressed his anger and frustration at his white teacher and other white children and young people. When he started listening to hip hop music and going around using 'gangsta' language it was extremely important to hold this, rather than try to control or criticise this behaviour. However, it did not take much for Utim to return to the Encounter stage (2), as he only had to get into trouble at school for this to happen. The difference now was that he had the space to verbalise and make visible his 'encounters' and explore this in our sessions.

There was no 'happy ever after' ending in my work with Utim and no clear movement into the *Internalisation stage* (4/5). This is the 'confident' stage of identity, often marked by the young person engaging with wider struggles and forming alliances with groups of people where there is mutual understanding and respect of identity and difference. Our work together was a mixture of positive aspects and some painful learning for both Utim and myself. Utim did begin to speak in Punjabi and also began to learn written Urdu—and this contributed to him feeling more confident and more in tune with his family and community. So there was some Internalisation but there was also ongoing movement between the Encounter, Immersion and Internalisation stages. Did he ever stop scrubbing his skin raw? Yes he did. But the healing, both physically and mentally, took a very long time.

JAMILA

Jamila was 15 years old when I first met her. She was a young woman who described herself as Black British. Her dual heritage was African-Caribbean and Indian. Jamila was in residential care in a predominantly white Children's Home. She was a very angry young woman and had been labelled as 'violent'. She had been 'looked after' since the age of ten and had been sexually abused by her father and later by a foster carer. Jamila had experienced three foster care placements that had broken down because of her behaviour. She had not had contact with family members for about two years. Jamila and I 'clicked' when we first met. My colour, hair and physical appearance were not dissimilar to Jamila's and this might have played a significant part in our relationship and interaction.

In exploring issues around her anger and the fact that she clearly carried recent scars of cutting herself, one of the recurring themes was being let down by social workers. She talked with a lot of anger about how she felt cheated by workers and blamed 'us' for where she was. When she talked about social workers she always used the word 'white' in a derogatory way. She would simply not engage with any questions about how she perceived me and often said things like 'you are not one of them'. With passion she shared her prior expectation that she would be protected by services but instead had been put in a 'strange environment', an environment where she was 'isolated and abused', not sexually but racially. She wanted to know why 'we' saw fit to place her in an environment which was totally white, without any sense of what it might feel like. Jamila was in the *Immersion stage* (3) as she was completely immersed in her sense of being different and being black. This stage can be both an angry and challenging stage and one where race is polarised—black is good and white is bad. Hence all social workers equated to being 'white', and this was possibly why she saw me as 'not one of them' and her refusal to engage in discussions of where I might be located within her experience of social workers.

In our sessions she began to open up about both her father and the foster carer's abuse and what it meant not having contact with any of her birth family. It was at this point that she began to compare being sexually abused with that of being racially abused. This was perhaps one of her *Encounter* (2) experiences, where the abuse shocked her sufficiently into being open to new ways of seeing herself. There was a tentative openness to explore what had happened to her and to embrace new ways of 'being'. This also shows how the identity model is not linear and 'encounters' can happen at various points in a person's life.

It was through my work with Jamila that I began to really understand that racial abuse is just as soul-destroying as sexual abuse and that there is no hierarchy in abuse. I was fortunate in some ways to come to the UK as an adult. For a black child born and growing up in the UK the experience is very different. I had a lot of good and strong memories and experiences to sustain me when facing racism but Jamila had very few. She told me that if she were given a choice she would go back home with her abusing father because 'at least I knew the signs when trouble was brewing' and she had no expectations of her family. By contrast, she explained that in the residential home she had made the mistake of believing that she would be safe.

Jamila talked about the bullying and name-calling she experienced on a daily basis—in the home, on the bus and in school. These were all further encounters—which contributed to her moving like a yo-yo between the *Encounter* (2) and *Immersion* (3) stages. This often intensified and reinforced her 'immersion'. There was something particularly poignant when she described being called 'a "Paki" all day and night' and having no peace. She told me that she could almost handle the name-calling and taunts. The thing that was most painful was when nobody would sit near her unless told to do so and that she never had anyone to play with. Her way of surviving was to read books all the time and write in her diary. She also learnt very quickly how to get attention and 'freak' people out. I needed to try and create some level of stability by supporting her to move into the *Internalisation stage* (4) where we could turn her anger into a sense of pride in herself. This would mean that she could be more outward-looking and no longer simply inward-looking and obsessed with how others might see or define her.

When we began work on exploring her cutting and why she did it, she was consistent in always saying that this did not stem from anger or frustration or pain. It simply was an act where she had to see the colour of her blood in order to remind herself and others that she was a human being and was 'the same as the rest of them'.

One way in which I encouraged Jamila to internalise her experiences and sense of self was by keeping a treasure box that contained all the positive things about her. We also spent time doing fun things like hair and skin care, eating out at culturally diverse restaurants and using henna to design patterns on her hands and/or feet and gradually developing this as an alternative to cutting. This internalisation of storing good strong memories was very necessary given the limitations within her pre-adolescence years where she had had little opportunity to explore different elements of her identity.

Jamila continues to remain in touch me. She is now a social worker and counsellor and has a relationship with her mother and her brothers. She still has no contact with her father. The last contact she had with him was when she was 18 years old. She had asked me to be with and support her, as she wanted to meet up with him. The meeting was very difficult but she very clearly told her father what she thought of him and why she would never have any kind of a relationship with him. This was a clear demonstration of Jamila having achieved the *Internalisation-Commitment* (5) stage where, through enhanced self-esteem, valuing herself and her identity, she was able to take control and be empowered in her interaction with her father.

IMPLICATIONS OF THE CROSS AND PARHAM MODEL

Reflecting on my work with Utim and Jamila helped me to acknowledge and understand that issues of identity can intersect with issues of violence and abuse and this in turn can result in self-harm. Experiences of violence and abuse are often multi-dimensional and complex. A range of factors influence the survival mechanisms adopted by young people. These include their developmental age; sense of identity and belonging; role in their family and wider society; economic and social positioning; social support networks; and the nature and frequency of violent and abusive relationships they have experienced. Hence it is essential to recognise the impact of such experiences, to understand and respect the ways in which the young person has found to survive these experiences, and to work with these sensitively and carefully. This involves recognising that survival strategies are *adaptive*, rather than being definitive and problematic. Dismantling something we have no real understanding of can lead to setting a young person adrift. It is often this need to 'rescue' young people from their self-harm that can sometimes cause the most damage to young people's survival mechanisms. This was something that I learnt and really struggled with, particularly in my work with Utim.

It is necessary to acknowledge that as the young person begins to make sense of their identity, the worker will almost definitely go through a similar kind of process. After some of my sessions with Utim and Jamila I carried with me an enormous anger that I struggled to channel. This is one example of why effective supervision and support of workers is absolutely crucial.

Although Cross originally conceptualised black identity as a linear process, my work with Utim, Jamila and other young people suggests otherwise. Cross' (1971) model has been criticised for its inability to engage with and recognise issues of class, gender, sexuality and disability, and that its linear process is too rigid and does not sufficiently reflect developmental process through adolescence. Such concerns led to Parham's modification of Cross' linear model into a more flexible one (Parham, 1989). He suggests that whilst the questioning of identity often begins in adolescence and early adulthood, it is a process that an individual can return to at different points in their lives. He also suggests that once *Internalisation-Commitment* (5) is achieved, it is not an absolute. New experiences might trigger the *Pre-Encounter* (1) and *Encounter* (2) stages or even the *Immersion/Emersion stage* (3). However, a weakness in Parham's view of black identity is the lack of recognition that an individual can be in a place where more than one of the stages co-exist:

> the most important advance Parham makes is that he puts forward
> a theory of the black person as a dynamic subject ... it is a theory of

subjectivity that moves some way beyond the linear stage model of black identity development ... However Parham does not address the 'possibility that multiple stages (or positions) may coexist within (or be available to) a given individual at a given moment'. (Mama, 1995, in Robinson 1998: 17)

The fact that more than one stage can co-exist was very evident in my experience of working with Utim and Jamila and contributes to the complexity and emotive nature of identity-based work. Parham also does not wholly acknowledge that different aspects of identity might begin at different developmental stages and almost certainly begins pre-adolescence. It is necessary to remember that identity development precedes adolescence. Parham (1989) uses an analogy of a 'storehouse' and suggests that pre-adolescent 'black identity' experiences are 'stored' until the child enters adolescence. He argues that it is at this point, when a young person 'encounters' issues related to their black identity, that experiences in the 'storehouse' come into focus. For example, both Utim and Jamila would have been storing their experiences of, perhaps, not being invited to birthday parties, being called names, and hearing derogatory comments etc. As younger children, they would have a more limited ability to process this information, other than having a sense of being different and unpopular. According to Parham, it is when they move into adolescence and perhaps get called a racist name that this 'encounter' would connect them with these 'stored-up' experiences. Clearly, pre-adolescents are able to make some of these connections, as evidenced by the use of self-harm by children as young as 7 years old (NCH & the Centre for Social Justice, Coventry University, 2002; MHF, 2006).

How children and young people understand and make sense of their oppression may change over time and will very often reflect the prevalent dominant values and experiences in their family, community and wider society. This suggests that the nature of the work done with pre-adolescent young people around identity might need to take particular shape dependent on the developmental stage of the child/young person and their political and social environment. It would focus on identifying and building on the positives with a view to balancing out the negatives accumulating in the storehouse. This kind of work might involve positive black images, eating out, getting involved in cultural activities and nurturing language development. In contrast, working and engaging with a young person in adolescence might involve building on and extending the 'storehouse' of positive experiences but would need to engage with the historical, social and political frameworks of race and racism.

CONCLUSIONS

I have made a case for viewing self-harm through the lens of models of identity formation. The Cross and Parham model has informed my work with black children and young people, but also with young people who use self-harm and who struggle with other aspects of their identity, for example, young people struggling with issues of sexuality, disability and young women who have been sexually abused (see Mama, 1995).

If we shift the nature of our work to a more explicit focus on identity (rather than purely self-harm) it can change the direction of our work. This is because it invites us to consider our responses to self-harm in the context of the possible influence of race and colour, or any other issues of structural oppression that inform identity. For example, what is the difference between a young black person scrubbing their skin raw or even bleaching it and a white young person who cuts him or herself? In many ways, it is not the 'action' itself that is different but the values and explanations we attach to it. Raising issues of identity more directly invites us to consider these values and explanations. Although it doesn't give us any easy answers, thinking about identity helps us to reintroduce notions of abuse and racism (or other oppressive and discriminatory acts) into discussions of self-harm because it moves the focus from the harm young people do to themselves, to the oppression that may underlie it.

REFERENCES

Cross, WE (1971) The Negro to black conversion experience: Towards the psychology of black liberation. *Black World, 20, 13–27.*

Cross, WE, Parham, TA & Helms, JE (1991) *The Stages of Black Identity Development: Nigrescence models.* Berkeley, CA: Cobb & Henry Publishers.

Gordon, P (1990) *Racial Violence and Harassment.* London: Runnymede Trust.

Lorde, A *(1988) A Burst of Light.* London: Sheba.

Mama, A *(1995) Beyond the Masks: Race, gender and subjectivity.* London: Routledge.

MHF (2006) *Truth Hurts—Report of the National Inquiry into Self-Harm among Young People.* London: Mental Health Foundation.

NCH & the Centre for Social Justice, Coventry University (2002) *Look beyond the Scars: Understanding and responding to self-harm.* London: NCH.

Parham, TA (1989) Cycles of psychological nigrescence. *The Counselling Psychologist 17,* 187–226.

Robinson, L (1998) *'Race', Communication and the Caring Professions.* Buckingham: Open University Press.

PART THREE:
STRATEGIES OF SURVIVAL

Chapter 9

SELF-HARM AND THE LAW:
WHAT CHOICES DO WE REALLY HAVE?

SAM WARNER AND DOUG FEERY

INTRODUCTION

Throughout this book it has been argued that self-harm is a means through which people sometimes manage feelings of powerlessness and distress. As such, according to this understanding, self-harm serves an adaptive function for the people who use it. As this understanding has become more widespread, service providers have had to adapt their practices in supporting people who self-harm. Hence, although some services are still rooted in a pathological model of mental illness that underpins a 'self-harm must be stopped' approach, many service providers now aim for more tolerance, understanding and flexibility. This means that increasingly self-harm is accepted as a legitimate coping strategy, and that harm minimisation strategies are preferable to, and more effective than, attempts to stop self-harm altogether. Hence, methods that reduce risk in self-harm may be promoted by service providers. For example, 'safer-cutting' kits (containing sterilised blades, antiseptic wipes etc) may be provided, and practical advice about safer self-harm may be given. In *In and Out of Harms Way* (Alex, 2006: 11), a booklet produced by 42nd Street, and developed by young people who self-harm, advice is given about 'keeping safe' whilst cutting, burning and overdosing.

Practices such as these are frequently validated by people who self-harm. But what status do they have in law, and what choices regarding self-harm are we, as service providers and users, legally entitled to make? This chapter explores some of the key aspects of British law that affect (young) people who self-harm, and those who work with them. The aim is to enable both service users and providers to have a better understanding of the legal consequences of self-harm. The chapter begins by demonstrating how the law restricts an individual's choice to use self-harm as a coping strategy. The impact of detention in prisons and under the Mental Health Act (DoH, 1983) is explored. Consideration is then given to the potentially positive impact of changes in how mental capacity is determined, and the potentially negative impact of the extension of compulsory powers under the Mental

Health Act (hereafter referred to as MHA). Finally, an argument is made for using advocates, lawyers and expert witnesses to secure people's choices and human rights regarding their lives and how they cope within them.

WHEN PERSONAL CHOICE BECOMES PUBLIC DEBATE: THE IMPACT OF INCARCERATION

For many adults and young people, self-harm is a private activity. What they do reflects their individual choice and represents their unique coping mechanisms. However, when people come into contact with public services, 'personal' choice becomes mediated by the 'professional' decisions of others. Whether someone is entitled to self-harm then becomes a matter for debate, and professionals (such as doctors, social workers, nurses, police, psychologists etc), depending on their particular role and remit in respect of the client, may contribute to this decision-making process. Supporting a client's right to self-harm becomes a moral, practical and ultimately legal issue, whereby professionals must balance risk (of harm to client and others) against charges of negligence (which might be brought against service providers). Hence, it is not simply about whether any individual is capable of making a decision about self-harm, but is also about whether the services that the individual is involved with could be judged negligent if they were deemed to support, or take insufficient measures to stop, self-harm.

Take the case of Mr Watkins.[1] Mr Watkins was a long time user of self-harm. Specifically, he found refuge in cutting his skin with razor blades. His use of self-harm, he said, was his only coping mechanism to escape the trauma of various life events that he found too harrowing to deal with in his mind. He was well known to the primary care authorities who, where possible, supported him in 'safer' options of self-harm. However, when Mr Watkins was sent to prison, he found the solitary environment an additional and major pressure, due largely to the limited number of distractions available to him. He asked prison officers to provide him with razor blades for the purposes of self-injury, but was refused. He argued that this infringed his 'human rights'[2] and that as he was not 'mentally disordered' and had 'full capacity' to make decisions about himself, he was entitled to make an informed choice about his self-harm. Despite his protests, no blades were provided and indeed he was subject to a greater level of observation. Mr Watkins challenged the

---

1. *Watkins* (Jeffrey) (R on the Application of) v. *Secretary of State for the Home Department*, Administrative Court. 6 April 2005.
2. Article 8, European Convention on Human Rights.

decision of the prison authorities by making an application to the High Court. The Court, whilst sympathetic to his case, refused to order that he be allowed access to razor blades for the purpose of self-harm. In fact the Court highlighted the necessity of the prison authorities to keep the prisoner safe from harm, as to do otherwise would mean that the prison officers would be negligent in their duty of care.

This case highlights that an individual may be recognised in law as being capable of making informed choices about whether or not to self-injure. However, whether the choice to self-harm is accepted, understood and/or supported will depend partly on where the self-harm takes place. Where such behaviour takes place in environments such as prisons, where professionals may not be understanding or sympathetic to the uses of self-harm, it will not be tolerated, regardless of whether or not it is a coping mechanism, lifestyle choice or otherwise. In the case of Mr Watkins, the prison authorities looked to the Court to legitimise their unease with self-harm. As such, a moral and practical concern was transformed into a legal decision that the judiciary took on behalf of the State.

What this means is that although service providers may want to support individual choice around self-harm, within certain contexts such as prisons (including young offender institutions), the law militates against this. This individual legal decision has, therefore, wider implications because it can be used as a landmark case that other services may refer to in order to clarify how they should work. Problems obviously arise because, just as mental health professional workers sometimes have insufficient understanding of the law, the judiciary sometimes has insufficient understanding of mental health issues and yet must make decisions about them. The result may be that people like Mr Watkins are doubly punished. First, they have their liberty taken away from them. Second, their usual coping strategies are denied them. This may ultimately serve to exaggerate and intensify the punishment they have been ascribed beyond that which may be deemed to be humane or fair. So, if the judiciary is poor at making judgements about mental health, how good can our existing mental health laws be? As signalled by the case of Mr Watkins, there are three key pieces of law that determine whether an individual, even when knowing the risks, sometimes should not be entitled to take them. The first is the Mental Health Act 1983 (MHA), the second is the Human Rights Act 1998 (HRA), and finally the Mental Capacity Act (DoH, 2005).[3]

---

3. The Mental Capacity Act 2005, not implemented until April 2007.

THE MENTAL HEALTH ACT AND MENTAL CAPACITY:
DECIDING WHO DECIDES

Over time, and with practice, people can become expert in self-harm, especially regarding their preferred method and its effects on their own body. Nevertheless, there are risks involved with any act of self-harm, and no method is entirely safe. Because the risks associated with different forms of self-harm fluctuate across people and occasions it may be too simplistic to support individuals to self-harm in all situations. For example, sometimes clients feel out of control of their self-harm and look to others to keep them safe. Conversely, sometimes others determine that the person who is self-harming is not 'in their right mind' and should be stopped from self-harming. Hence, the right to self-harm is not universal, nor unchallengeable. This is evident, as indicated, for those detained in prisons and young offender institutions, and also for those who have been subject to detention under the MHA (1983). The principles that underpin the MHA are as follows:

> No adult citizen of the United Kingdom is liable to be confined in any institution against his will, save by the authority of law. That is a fundamental constitutional principle, traceable back to Ch. 29 of Magna Carta 1297 (25 Edw. 1 c 1), and before that to Ch. 39 of Magna Carta (1215). There are, of course, situations in which the law sanctions detention. The most obvious is in the case of those suspected or convicted of crime. Powers then exist to arrest and detain. But the conditions in which those powers may be exercised are very closely prescribed by statute and the common law ... [Mental patients] present a special problem since they may be liable, as a result of mental illness, to cause injury either to themselves or to others. But the very illness which is the source of the danger may deprive the sufferer of the insight necessary to ensure access to proper medical care, whether the proper medical care consists of assessment or treatment, and, if treatment, whether in patient or out patient treatment. Powers therefore exist to ensure that those who suffer from mental illness may, in appropriate circumstances, be involuntarily admitted to mental hospitals and detained. (Sir Thomas Bingham M.R.)[4]

In short, the MHA provides for the liberty of an individual to be curtailed where they are understood to be suffering from a mental disorder that requires assessment and/or treatment. In the words of the Court of Appeal:

---

4. *Re S-C (Mental patient: Habeas Corpus)* [1996] 1 All E.R. 532, CA, at 534, 535.

[The] policy and objects of this Act are to regulate the circumstances in which the liberty of persons who are mentally disordered may be restricted and, where there is conflict, to balance their interests against those of public policy.[5]

People in the community, where they are in receipt of statutory mental health and social care services, have *some* choice regarding whether they self-harm. Yet, once detained under the MHA (1983), their choices may become as restricted as those persons in prisons (like Mr. Watkins) and young offender institutions. The relationship between involuntary detention under the MHA and the practice of self-harm is not, however, straightforward. Self-harm, in and of itself, does not lead to someone being assessed for admission to hospital under the MHA. This is because self-harm/self-injurious behaviour, in and of itself, does not constitute a mental disorder within the meaning of the MHA. What the self-harming behaviour does do, however, is draw attention to the individual, and invites others to ask questions regarding why that individual self-harms. The dilemma that then ensues is what understanding professionals place on the behaviour when considering it, and applying it, to a legal definition, namely, 'is there a mental disorder?' As noted, in the above extract from the judgement of Sir Thomas Bingham, he says:[6]

[Mental patients] present a special problem since they may be liable, as a result of mental illness, to cause injury either to themselves or to others.

Self-harm may therefore fall into this definition. Hence, even when the reasons for self-harm are understood and accepted by the individual and the relevant professionals, the act of self harm may still lead to the individual being detained. Once detained, additional rules come into play that circumscribe self-harming behaviour in hospitals. The Code of Practice relating to the MHA (1983) provides the following:

Patients must be protected from harming themselves when the drive to self-injury is a result of mental disorder for which they are receiving care and treatment. On admission, all patients should be assessed for immediate and potential risks of going missing, suicide, self-harm and self-neglect, taking into account their social and clinical history.

---

5. (Ibid.)
6. (Ibid.)

Individual care plans should include:
• A clear statement of the degree of risk of self-harm.
• The measures required to manage risk safely.
• The level of observation needed to ensure the patient's safety.

Staff must balance the potentially distressing effect on the patient of close observation, particularly when one-to-one observation is proposed for many hours, against the risk of self-injury. (Department of Health & Welsh Office, 1999 [my italics])

This quote makes clear that where the individual is diagnosed as suffering from a mental disorder, which has been determined as requiring detention under the MHA (1983), then she/ he will not be allowed to self-harm. The Code of Practice clearly requires her/him to be stopped (see italicised portion of text). Although the Code of Practice for the MHA (1983) is guidance, and hence any recommendations should not be mandatory, that was not the view taken by the Court of Appeal.[7] The view taken by the Court was that whilst it was merely guidance, it must be followed unless there were exceptional reasons for departing from it. This judgement endorses an existing controlling culture in statutory care, and undermines more creative practices.

The need to exert control over people who self-harm may be further reinforced when self-harm is determined to infer suicidal intent. For example, Article 2 of European Convention on Human Rights,[8] sets out the 'right to life'. Foster (2003) notes that recently a coroner's court case confirmed that service failure to prevent suicide amounted to negligence.[9] Hence, this may encourage workers (in the community as well) to 'cover their backs', by treating all self-harm as if it were suicidal in intent. This reinforces restrictive practices with all clients who self-harm, even though increased control over detainees and others is frequently associated with greater incidents of self-harm (Warner & Wilkins, 2004). Unfortunately, legal directives may then functionally override clinical judgement, as the main consideration becomes 'is this self-harm legal?' Rather than 'is this self-harm useful?'

Detained mental health patients clearly have a reduced set of rights in relation to what they can do with their own bodies. This is because the MHA (1983) rests on the assumption that those detained under it have insufficient insight to make judgements about their own actions, and hence need others to do so on their behalf. It may well be the case that people have different

---

7. *Munjaz* v. *Mersey Care NHS Trust* and *S* v. *Airedale NHS Trust* [2003] EWCA Civ 1036 – Paragraph 19.30–19.31.
8. Enshrined in domestic law through the Human Rights Act 1998.
9. *R* v. *HM Coroner for NW London ex p Scott*, 13.2.01.

capacities to make reasoned judgements about themselves at different times in their lives. Nevertheless, it is still possible to enable people to exert some control over their lives and bodies even when they may be (temporarily) mentally incapacitated. A written 'advance directive' (Amering et al., 1999) can be used to outline what particular clients need during points of crisis, when their capacity to understand and/or articulate their needs themselves is compromised. For people who have mental health problems, this means that advance directives can be drawn up when people's mental capacity to think about themselves is robust, to be used at times when their mental capacity may be less reliable.

According to the Drug and Therapeutics Bulletin (DTB, 1997), advance directives, in mental health, may apply to treatment for a mental disorder up to a point. People may determine their own treatment, *unless* the treatment is one that can be given without consent under the MHA (1983). The use of advance directives can be an important tool in formalising clients' needs and wishes. And, if clients' needs are responded to more appropriately, this may go some way to avoiding their ultimate detention under the MHA (1983). At the heart of debates about when the MHA comes into effect (and hence when advance directives may be ignored) is the issue of mental capacity: lack of which can result in involuntary detention. The relationship between the MHA and judgements about mental capacity are changing, however.

A new Mental Capacity Act (DoH, 2005) is due to come into force in April 2007, and will apply to adults aged 16 years and over. According to this new Act, professionals will have to *prove* lack of capacity, rather than *assume* incapacity because an individual has a mental health diagnosis. This new Act has arisen, in part, because of concerns that even when the MHA (1983) was not used to detain people, people who were accommodated in their 'best interests' under the common law doctrine of 'necessity' had their rights undermined too. Specifically the 'right to liberty' is undermined by making too many assumptions about mental incapacity.[10] As such, those who provide inpatient services to adults judged to lack capacity need to carefully consider the basis on which they do so, as the law in respect of capacity is changing.

According to the new Mental Capacity Act (DoH, 2005) the following statutory principles are to be implemented. The first, as indicated, is the 'assumption of capacity', which means that every adult (16 years and over) has the right to make his/her own decisions and must be assumed to have capacity to do so, unless proved otherwise. In addition, people should not be presumed to lack capacity because of a particular diagnosis. Second, people must also be

---

10. See *R* v. *Bournewood Community and Mental Health NHS Trust, ex parte L* (HL) 1998 3 WLR 107 *The Times* June 30th.

given all appropriate support to make their own decisions before it is concluded they lack capacity. Third, individuals retain the right to make what might seem to be 'unwise' decisions. Finally, if an individual is deemed to lack capacity, anything done on their behalf must be done in their 'best interests' and should be the 'least restrictive alternative'. Hence, detention would be the last resort. However, in cases where the MHA (1983) *is* deemed necessary, this would override the proposed Mental Capacity Act, at least in relation to the 'condition' for which the MHA (1983) is being used. It is unclear what this may mean for a patient detained under the MHA in relation to his/her 'right' to self-harm—this may need judicial clarification through a test case.

For those under 16 years of age, the situation in respect of determining capacity, and its effects, is slightly different. It is still the understanding and intelligence of the individual child that determines whether she/he has the capacity to, and therefore can give, consent to medical treatment including that for matters of mental health. And consent by a competent minor cannot be overridden by a parent's refusal. However, the reverse does not apply. As the DTB (1997: 42) notes:

> [A] minor's refusal to consent to treatment will not be binding where the parent(s) give valid consent for treatment to go ahead, but this must be in the child's best interest ... This position may seem illogical in that the right to consent is worthless if unaccompanied by the right to refuse.

The argument is that doctors need the right to provide treatment with certainty (ibid.). Yet there are sometimes serious problems regarding the relationship between young people and their parents. A significant number of young people who self-harm have experienced neglectful parenting and/or physical, emotional and sexual abuse (Women at the Margins, 2004). When children have experienced abuse by the people who care for them, and they come into the care of the Local Authority, 'parental responsibility' may transfer to the State, which acts as the de facto 'nearest relative'. This is important because otherwise parents continue to determine what happens to children, by virtue of being able to give consent to treatment as the 'nearest relative'. Additionally, under the MHA (1983) the nearest relative has a significant role in relation to detention for adults too.

For example, if the nearest relative objects to an application for treatment (under Section 3, MHA, 1983) admission cannot occur unless a county court order displaces him or her as the nearest relative (Foster, 2003). 'Respect for privacy and family life' (Article 8 of the Human Rights Act, 2000) maintains the need for a nearest relative. However, the Government has made a commitment to review this aspect of law, precisely because the nearest relative does not always act in the person's best interests. As such, some changes have already been made to how the nearest relative is defined. For example, the High Court has determined[11] that, in order to comply with Article 8, 'living as husband and wife' must include same-sex partners (Foster, 2003).

The choices individuals can make about their treatment, in respect of issues associated with their self-harm (which might include both their mental and physical health) may be subject to familial, as well as professional, intervention. How the MHA (1983) is applied and how mental capacity is understood, to some degree, determines just how much others can be involved in this decision-making process. Although detention under the MHA serves to restrict people's choices about self-harm and their treatment, at least they can appeal against detention. If they are successful, such people reassert their choices around self-harm and treatment (they can make more choices in the community). As the aforementioned Bournewood case (see Footnote 10) suggests, 'informally' detained patients have no such legal rights. However, the choices people can currently make about their self-harm and their treatment in the community is being eroded. In the future, people in the community, like people detained in hospital, may also be made subject to mandatory treatment.

A controversial draft Mental Health Bill was abandoned recently after eight years of planning. Sustained criticism from mental health charities, civil rights groups and mental health/service user activists centred on concerns that patients' rights would be (further) undermined by proposed changes that extended compulsory powers. Unfortunately, although the Bill was defeated, the push to extend compulsory powers has not gone away. The proposal now is to amend existing mental health laws. Proposed measures include forcing patients to comply with community treatment orders or face detention. This may have a direct and negative impact on patients in the community who choose to self-harm because, for example, their consultant determines that 'treatment' should include stopping self-harm. Further, if treatment is mandated in the community this means that patients may find that related choices are also restricted. This is not only in terms of medication they may be forced to take, but also in terms of other forms of therapy, including talking therapies.

At the moment, choice about talking therapies can be constructively denied because professionals determine what services clients have access to, and the form these services take. If compulsory treatment includes talking

---

11. *R* (on the application of SSG) v. *Liverpool City Council, the Secretary of State for Health ad LS* (Interested Party), unreported, October 22, 2002.

therapies (as well as use of medication), it may be that service users in the future will be mandated into forms of psychotherapy they do not want and which ultimately undermine them. As argued in Chapter 1 for example, cognitive behavioural forms of psychotherapy predominate in the National Health Service because they have simple goals that are amenable to formal measurement (and so can be 'proved'), and are short term (and hence, economical) in focus. Yet service users may not want to be corralled into accepting these forms of treatment, as is often the case with approaches such as 'dialectical behaviour therapy'. However, just because a therapy method is easy to follow (such as self-harm is not to be 'reinforced'), and its outcomes easy to measure (such as cessation of self-harm) this does not make that method *the* treatment of choice. Changes in mental health legislation should not be used to promote 'easily evidenced' therapies and restrict access to more user-friendly services that cater to individual need. One model seldom fits all. So, service users who are unhappy with the forms of treatment (physical, social, medical and/or psychological) that are provided within the area they live may find their choices narrowing in the future.

Yet, not all legislation is restrictive. Some aspects of the law do promote individual rights.

HUMAN RIGHTS AND LEGAL CHOICES: USING ADVOCATES, LAWYERS AND EXPERT WITNESSES

As noted, young people who self-harm and do not come into contact with statutory services (those who, in effect, self-harm in private) have some freedom to do as they wish with their bodies. However, isolation can contribute to negative mental health and restrict opportunities for developing good relationships that might mediate negative emotions and the need to self-harm. It is important, therefore, that privacy is a choice, rather than isolation being an effect of inadequate and inappropriate service provision. If young people are not to be ignored, then they may need help to find and engage in services they want. There is a range of ways in which young people's choices around self-harm, and other life issues, can be supported.

Independent advocacy services exist, both in community and secure care settings, and are there to promote the views of the people they represent. For example, when young people exhibit 'risky' behaviour, such as repetitive self-harm, 'risk management' meetings may be held on a regular basis to review the young person's behaviour and the services provided to them. Such meetings are attended by all the significant people involved in the young person's care. This may include the psychiatrist, psychologist, key workers, social worker etc, as well as the young person him/herself. It is not always easy for the client to feel fully able to represent their views in such meetings, and an independent advocate can help with this process. As advocates are independent to service providers, they are free to promote the young person's perspective, and are free to seek external advice on the young person's behalf. They may use documents, such as the aforementioned advance directives, that can further describe the person's point of view. However, as noted, advance directives are not binding, and whilst statutory services must take into account the service user's views, they do not have to follow them.

When a significant breakdown occurs between a service user and the service, the only remedy may be a legal one. As such, it is important that people who self-harm have some basic understanding of their legal rights. Citizens' Advice Bureaux are good places to start, as they can give information, advice and also identify local legal services. It is important to find good legal representation as, ultimately, legal advocates are the people who will argue their case, at Mental Health Tribunals, in family courts etc. Increasingly, people are turning to the Human Rights Act (1998), which was incorporated into the law of Scotland in 1999, and England and Wales in 2000 (hereafter referred to as HRA). This Act, alluded to earlier, serves additional functions to existing social care and mental health legislation, and has been used to force changes in how people with mental health problems have been treated. For example, the HRA has been used to change the basis of detention under the 1983 Mental Health Act (MHA).

Under section 72 (and where relevant S.73) of the MHA (1983) a detained patient has the responsibility of satisfying the mental health tribunal that he/she is *not* in need of detention—notwithstanding the burden of proof being on the detaining authority (DoH 2001).[12] This is rather than the hospital needing to prove the patient *needs* detention. However, according to Article 5 of the HRA (1998) 'everyone has the right to liberty and security of person'. As such the Court of Appeal[13] determined that making patients prove they did not need detention was incompatible with the HRA. The Government has remedied this by shifting the 'burden of proof' to the hospital (see Foster, 2003), which must now demonstrate any ongoing need to detain patients. Additionally, also under Article 5, a case was made that there is a need for periodic reviews of detained persons and that repeated cancellations of tribunals violated patients rights[14] (ibid.).

---

12. See MHA 1983 [Remedial] Order 2001 (S.I. 2001. No. 3712) [Effective 26.11.01].
13. In *R* (H) v. *MHRT, North West Region*, 2001, 28 March.
14. See the landmark Judgement of the Honourable Justice Stanley-Burton in the case of *R* (on the application of KB) v. *Mental Health Review Tribunal* [2002] EWHC 639, (2002) 5 C.C.L. Rep. 458; [2002] A.C.D. 85; (2002) 152 N.L.J. 672, QBD (Admin).

The HRA (1998) has, therefore, been used to force progressive changes in the ways that other existing legislation, such as the MHA (1983) is applied. Other aspects of this Act have also been used to challenge restrictive practices. For example, under Article 3 'inhuman or degrading treatment' is forbidden and this aspect of the HRA (1998) can be used to raise objections to different forms of treatment (including medical, social and psychological). However, this process is not straightforward. Foster (ibid: 3) draws attention to the judgement of the Court of Appeal,[15] which 'indicated that the mental capacity of the patient to understand treatment options would be important in deciding whether forcing treatment upon him or her violated his/her Article 3 rights'. It is as yet unclear how changes in how we understand mental capacity in law will affect decisions such as these.

It is evident that the HRA (1998) is not a panacea for the wrongs of other laws. However, it does provide an additional avenue for challenging bad practice under the MHA (1983) and also in respect of wider issues under family law, for example, that may additionally affect young people who self-harm. Claims that are made under the HRA (1998) do not necessarily lead to changes in practice—the court cannot enforce recommendations. However, petitions brought under the Act can be used to halt changes in service provision, whilst the court is in proceedings. Ultimately, court proceedings force those who wish to change services to justify their actions before a judge. This is important because it means that decisions about treatment cannot be taken behind closed doors where the outcome will, and does, directly affect the individual. In order to assist the judge in making decisions about an individual's social well-being and mental health, an 'expert witnesses' may be appointed to provide an opinion about the issue under review.

Some progressive professionals avoid court work because they do not want to act as 'agents of the State'. Yet, if we do not work with the law, we leave service users dependent on professionals who may not follow a progressive agenda (Warner, in press). Sometimes experts are called to offer evidence that challenges other expert evidence. In child and family proceedings, however, the expert has to be agreed by all the parties who are represented (including, for example, the young person, each parent, the Local Authority etc.), and is therefore jointly instructed. This means that the evidence provided by the expert cannot be suppressed by one party simply because they do not like it. Once the expert is agreed, the subsequent report is available to all. Expert testimony carries a large weight in enabling judges, and sometimes juries, to make sense of the issues laid before the court, and hence how this

---

15. *R* (on the application of Wilkinson) v. *RMO, Broadmoor Hospital and others*; [2001]. EWCA Civ 1545, [2002] 1 WLR 419; *The Times*, 2 November 2001.

will affect the service user. And although the opinion of the expert should be treated as opinion and not fact, the court still tends follow the recommendations of the expert witness (Richman et al, 2002). The extent of their influence may increase further.

For example, the Government has recently recommended that experts be used to explain to jurors the effects of rape (Branigan & Dyer, 2006), because of extremely low conviction rates. In effect, the Government is advocating a form of 'social framework evidence' (Raitt & Zeedyk, 2000). This approach derives from the idea that it is difficult to be objective about the judgements we make when what we know is made up of prejudice and selective information. We understand more when we have a clear and explicit framework through which to make sense of the information presented. This is where expert witnesses can help, by providing a richer and more detailed framework for understanding (Warner, in press). This is not just in respect of rape but also regarding issues of mental health and self-harm.

For example, rather than depicting self-harm as a symptom of mental disorder, such as borderline personality disorder, reports can 'frame' self-harm as a coping strategy. In this way, people's behaviour can be reassessed as being meaningful and helpful. As such, expert witness reports can function as a type of 'advance directive', in terms of detailing what works and does not work for the client, and what would help them in the future. They have, therefore, a potential educational function, which could contribute to greater understanding, and more helpful treatment, in law, mental health and social care practice, of people who self-harm.

LOOKING FOR LEGAL REMEDIES

There are many factors that contribute to how young people who self-harm are understood and treated. The law, like any other factor, is neither wholly good nor wholly bad. Different aspects of law undermine the rights of individuals, just as other aspects aim to secure those rights. It is evident that current mental health legislation, and that which covers people involuntarily detained (in prison or hospital), works to restrict the ability of people to utilise self-harm as a coping strategy that preserves life. This is partially because self-harm is too often, in law and practice, taken to be indicative of suicidal intent. It is crucial, therefore, that differences of intent (between coping and suicide) are mapped, as these require different, if sometimes overlapping, strategies and interventions. Advocates, and progressive lawyers and expert witnesses, can help this process in legal settings by ensuring that self-harm is understood as a strategy, that can be used with intent, rather than being simply a symptom of mental illness or personality disorder.

The social frameworks we draw on to understand self-harm, and matters of mental health, shape our practices. This is why it is crucial that the perspectives offered in this book are used to reframe the ways the law has traditionally understood (young) people who self-harm. People who self-harm deserve a just and fair legal system that preserves rights, rather than too quickly undermining personal control. The law changes and evolves precisely because people question it. The public arena of court is an important space in which individuals can renegotiate how their private acts of self-harm are understood and treated, and as such, this is a crucial place in which they may take back ownership of their lives.

REFERENCES

Alex (2006) *In and Out of Harm's Way*. Manchester: 42nd Street.

Amering, M, Stastny, P & Hopper, K (1999) Psychiatric advanced directives: Qualitative study of informed deliberations by mental health service users. *British Journal of Psychiatry 186*, 247–52.

Branigan, T & Dyer, C (2006) Sex violence policy has failed—minister. *The Guardian*, 13th March 2006, 1–3.

Department of Health (1983) *The Mental Health Act 1983*. London: Department of Health.

Department of Health (2001) *Remedial Order*. London: Department of Health.

Department of Health (2005) *The Mental Capacity Act 2005*. London: Department of Health.

Department of Health & Welsh Office (1999) *Code of Practice: The Mental Health Act 1983*. London: The Stationery Office.

Drug and Therapeutics Bulletin (1997) Managing self-harm: The legal issues. *Drug and Therapeutics Bulletin 35*, 41–3.

Foster, S (2003) The Human Rights Act and Mental Health. *MIND*, Internet Publication: MIND.

Raitt, FE & Zeedyk, S (2000) *The Implicit Relation of Psychology and Law: Women and syndrome evidence*. London: Routledge.

Richman, J, Berry, M & Hooper, J (2002) The role of British psychologists acting as expert witnesses: Myths and realities. Paper presented at the *New Laws for Forensic Psychology Conference*, November 11, Manchester Metropolitan University.

Warner, S (in press) *Understanding Women and Child Sexual Abuse: Feminist revolutions in theory, research and practice*. London: Psychology Press.

Warner, S & Wilkins, T (2004) Between subjugation and survival: Women, borderline personality disorder and high security mental hospitals. *Journal of Contemporary Psychotherapy, 34* (3), 265–78.

Women at the Margins (2004) Bullshit Psychiatric Diagnosis: Women at the margins: Women and borderline personality disorder. *Special edition of Asylum: The magazine for democratic psychiatry, 14* (3).

Chapter 10

WEAVING DIFFERENT PRACTICES: WORKING WITH CHILDREN AND YOUNG PEOPLE WHO SELF-HARM IN PRISON

Carolyn McQueen

I first began working with people who self-harm in Rampton, a high security mental hospital in the UK. I encountered women who were detained under the Mental Health Act (1983) because of risk of harm to themselves or others. Many of them hurt themselves deliberately. Most of them were young, between 19 and 25 years of age. The stories I heard were ones of pain, struggle, determination and survival. These women challenged my preconceptions about deliberate self-harm and have influenced how I work today. There are many reasons why people choose to hurt themselves. My work is not to make assumptions, but to sit with the individual and explore what would be useful to them. This may be to help them make sense of the self-harm or to find other, less destructive ways to survive, or maybe to acknowledge with them that all they can do at this moment is manage the best way they know, even if that means hurting themselves.

More recently I have worked with young men in a young offenders' institution. The stories I heard were familiar: self-harm was sometimes a way to survive, sometimes a way to resist, sometimes a release, sometimes a way to protest, and sometimes an avowal of life in the midst of much inhumanity. The response of the prison system could be extreme and often inhumane. And yet there were individual staff who were committed to working with these young people to improve their well-being, despite the constraints of the system. Here I outline some of my knowledge of forensic systems and argue how particular discourses within British society legitimise and structure juvenile imprisonment and create a regime in which self-harm flourishes. By drawing upon my own and colleagues' clinical experiences I illustrate how health professionals and workers from voluntary organisations can work to make a positive difference for young people who self-harm in prison.

SELF-HARM IN YOUNG OFFENDER INSTITUTIONS

Self-harm amongst juvenile and young offenders who are held in prison is a major concern for the Prison Service, health services and organisations such as the Howard League for Penal Reform that seek to change the way young offenders are dealt with. For example, figures show that in six months from November 2001, 322 incidents of self-harm took place in two Young Offender Institutions in Britain, involving 153 individuals (Howard League, 2003). In 2004, the rate of self-harm amongst young offenders was 198 per 1000 head of population (Howard League, 2006). Methods of self-harm included hanging, self-strangulation and cutting/scratching.

To understand how this situation has arisen, we need to understand the context in which children and young people are incarcerated and the ideas and ethics that lie behind it, as these profoundly influence the prison settings these children are sent to. The result is a culture where punishment predominates over rehabilitation. For children who are vulnerable, and already using self-harm to cope with difficult feelings and experiences, the environment is one where self-harming behaviour can increase as the need to cope increases. For other children it may be that to physically inflict pain on themselves in a very visible way is one way to aggressively resist an aggressive system. Although there have been major prison and government initiatives to tackle levels of self-harm in prisons, the prison regime itself constrains the ways in which health professionals and voluntary organisations can work with children and young people. This context presents particular dilemmas of practice that would rarely be encountered in the community.

SENDING CHILDREN TO PRISON

In Britain we incarcerate more children than any other country in Europe. Despite recommendations from organisations such as the Howard League for Penal Reform and the Children's Society, the practice continues. Prison Service figures showed a 36 per cent increase in custodial sentences for children between 1992 and 2001. Over the same period the rate of children remanded in custody rose by 142 per cent (NACRO, 2003). Media portrayals of young people today abound with how children are 'out of control' and in need of a 'short, sharp shock'. The Anti Social Behaviour Order (ASBO) is a dominant part of government policy on youth crime and contributes to very visible ideas that young people as a group are 'a problem'. When children transgress societal norms in extreme ways they are imbued with the attributes of adults, with fully developed cognitive and emotional functioning. For example, whenever a child is murdered by another child there are apparent widespread views that the child who has committed the murder is inherently evil, and should be incarcerated for life. Scant public attention is paid to the processes by which a child has come to act in these ways. The current political climate of being seen to be 'tough on crime' and the use of a strict disciplinarian approach to 'cure' offending sets up a context that informs not only the sentencing practices of the courts but also the day-to-day workings of prisons.

Children who are convicted of offences and given custodial sentences are the responsibility of the Youth Justice Board. Three types of accommodation comprise the Juvenile Secure Estate: Local Authority Secure Children's Homes (LASCH), Secure Training Centres (STCs) and Young Offender Institutions. LASCHs are used to house young offenders between the ages of 12 and 14 years, girls up to the age of 16 and boys aged 15–16 who have been assessed as vulnerable. Secure Training Centres (STCs) provide accommodation for young offenders up to the age of 17 years. They are purpose-built institutions run by private companies and have a focus on education and rehabilitation. They are meant to provide secure accommodation for 'vulnerable' young offenders.

The final option is to be sent to a Young Offender Institution. These are run by the Prison Service and provide accommodation for 15–21 year olds. Although termed 'institutions' they have been structured on the model used for adult prisons. The physical environment is one where external trappings of security predominate, from iron gates, barbed wire sitting atop wire fences, to (mainly) uniformed staff with visible key chains. Although juvenile offenders are housed in separate juvenile wings, the regulations of the wider Prison Service still apply.

CHILDREN AND YOUNG PEOPLE, SELF-HARM AND THE PRISON REGIME: AN OVERVIEW

Despite the Youth Justice Board's assertion that prisons should not be used to accommodate 'more vulnerable young offenders', the evidence suggests that these more vulnerable children and young people *do* end up in prison. Research shows that a high percentage of children in the prison system have mental health problems, histories of trauma, and many have been in the care system (Golding et al., 2006; Mental Health Foundation, 2002; Warren, 1999).

Many of the problematic histories experienced by children and young people in prisons parallel those of children and young people in the community who self-harm. These include sexual or physical abuse, witnessing violence within the family home, bereavement, bullying, experiencing a lack of support or communication (Babiker & Arnold, 1997, Godsi, 2004). The difference is in the day-to-day reality of their environments. Obviously both groups experience difficulties and conflict, yet the prison setting provides a unique combination of circumstances and relationships. Prisons require young people to find ways to cope that may bring them into direct conflict with the system in which they live.

Prisoners have reported several problems that may lead to self-harming within the prison setting (Howard League, 1999). A major problem for young people and children who are sent to prison is living in an intimidating environment in which they are subject to a hierarchical system of control. The control is not just the formally sanctioned rules, policies and procedures of the Prison Service, but also the informal, unwritten and culturally sanctioned ways of controlling groups of people (Foucault, 1977). A hierarchical system of power exists within the prison. Those holding particular positions of power, for example, prison officers, are able to impose official sanctions on prisoners who transgress rules of the institution. However, amongst prisoners, there is also a hierarchical system of power or 'pecking order' that is recognised (and spoken about) by both staff and prisoners. In this arena those prisoners with more standing (for example, gang leaders; those convicted of 'more prestigious' offences including armed robbery; or those that use physical and verbal intimidation within the prison to get their way) are afforded more respect. But bullying and intimidation occur not only between inmates but also between staff members, as well as from staff to prisoners. In this way particular behaviours are encouraged or discouraged by a more pervasive fear of the consequences of transgressing the unwritten rules and thus becoming an 'outsider'.

Although the Prison Service has anti-bullying strategies in place throughout its prisons, the problems still continue and have recently been highlighted in a report by Lord Carlisle commissioned by the Howard League (2006), as well as ongoing reports by HM Inspector of Prisons into individual prisons. Moreover, although anti-bullying policies may achieve a level of success between prisoners, unless there is successful management of bullying between staff and of prisoners by staff, then the system will be maintained. The consequent environment is potentially one of fear and aggression in which both staff and prisoners have to find a way to survive. For those young people who are already struggling with making sense of past experiences, a mix of emotions such as fear, anger and powerlessness may lead to an increased frequency of self-harm behaviours.

As self-harm is such a major concern for the Prison Service, new initiatives have been instigated by the Government to address the ever increasing levels of self-harm and suicide amongst prisoners (NIMHE, 2004). The Government has tried to address this by encouraging the collaborative working of the Prison Service with the Department of Health and the National Institute for Mental Health in England. Emerging from this has been the development of Mental Health 'In-Reach' Services to provide mental health services for prisoners within the prison system. In 2005 the Prison Service introduced the ACCT Approach for assessment of risk of suicide. This approach highlights Assessment, Care in Custody and Teamwork to manage prisoners who are self-harming or expressing thoughts of harming or killing themselves. The approach is multi-disciplinary and encourages staff to talk with and listen to prisoners, regularly assessing the risk of suicide. However, the danger is that within an overcrowded, understaffed prison system it can easily become a 'paper' exercise, with little impact on practice. Prison staff have little training in mental health and low morale is pervasive throughout the institutions. A culture of blame exists within the system so that when deaths in custody do occur, or young people severely injure themselves, prison staff feel that they alone will be held accountable. Not surprisingly, the management of self-harm becomes defensive, with the priority for the Prison Service being to stop the self-harming behaviour by whatever means (Howard League, 2001).

The defensive practices towards self-harm traditionally adopted by the Prison Service are further complicated by the fact that the Prison Service and prison governors have key performance indicators that include reducing levels of suicide within individual institutions. This is clearly about 'duty of care' to prisoners but the enmeshing of self-harm and suicide makes it difficult to change practice at an operational level. Prison governors also have ultimate control of how individual young people are managed within the institution, even if this is contrary to the advice of mental health professionals. This alone encourages more defensive practices in terms of reducing risk, compared to community settings where service users might be encouraged to use 'safer cutting' for example. The hierarchical system of control within prisons and the need to meet key Prison Service targets ultimately supports the actual physical restraint of self-harm by the use of body-belts, safe-clothing and segregation.

WEAVING DIFFERENT PRACTICES: WORKING CONSTRUCTIVELY WITH SELF-HARM IN PRISON

Given some of the difficulties and tensions of the prison regime, it is not surprising that workers are faced with considerable dilemmas when trying to work in prisons with young people who self-harm. They are entering what is, in the main, a punitive system, whose priority is security, and where there remains a predominant view of self-harm as attention-seeking and manipulative. The procedures that come into play when a young person harms him/herself in prison often lead to isolation, shame, boredom, feelings of helplessness, hopelessness and the construction of an identity limited to the self-harm.

Within such a context, the question could be asked: 'what can professionals and outside agencies offer a young person in such institutions?' The answer, I believe, lies in recognising that all arenas (including 'the community') present constraints and tensions for workers. In prisons, power dynamics and control issues are explicit and professionals have to find ways to work with those tensions that are beneficial to the young person. In my experience this can occur at an individual, or systemic level, or both, depending on the position of the individual worker (or their organisation) within individual institutions.

The following sections explore the different levels at which we can work with young people in prison, depending on contexts and relationships.

DEALING WITH THE PHYSICAL ENVIRONMENT

Prisoners live in cells. 'Juveniles' (under 16 years) have their own cell that usually has its own toilet and washbasin. They are allowed some of their own items within the cell (for example, duvet cover, posters, photos etc.) if they are not on a basic prison regime. 'Young offenders' (17–22 years) are likely to have to share a cell. The more vulnerable a young person's mental health is deemed to be by the Prison Service, the more likely they are to be 'paired up' to share a cell. This is thought to reduce the risk of self-harm or suicide. However, this is a complex situation. Although it may help some young people, it can be problematic for those who find it difficult to be around peers because of past abusive relationships. Furthermore, young people who self-harm to release tension or cope with the environment may not want to self-harm in front of someone, particularly someone they do not know. This may be because of feelings of shame associated with the behaviour, the need or desire to follow specific rituals they have developed on their own around their self-harm, or merely because they know that prison officers are almost certainly going to be called upon to intervene. Often such young people are acutely aware of the scars they carry on their bodies and resist wearing short sleeves or having showers, where there is little privacy from other prisoners. Consequently, they not only experience increased levels of anxiety and powerlessness, but their 'different' behaviour makes them more visible to the main prison population. This can lead to bullying and stigmatisation.

The shared cell is a difficult situation for workers to change. Prison officers conduct the risk assessments that determine cell allocation and beliefs that self-harm automatically means suicidal intent may predominate. Staff on the prison wing want the young person to be safe, and also, themselves, need to feel safe with the decisions they make within the system. Depending on their position within the prison, health professionals can contribute to the risk assessment, highlighting how sharing may actually increase the risk self-harm for some young people. They can also suggest that the young person themself has some degree of control in the process. For example, is there someone she would like to share with, or feel safe with? Health professionals, by having good relationships with prison staff, being seen to collaborate and to understand the tensions involved, and sharing the risk, can help support changes in practice in prisons.

Often prisons with a healthcare centre are able to provide private showers for prisoners who do not want to shower in the open showers on the wings. Workers can liaise with healthcare staff to arrange this. Prison staff on the wing may also support this, arranging for a young person to access the shower first or last, or at times of day when there are fewer prisoners out of their cells. In my experience this depends upon individual prison officers, some of whom have a greater understanding of the issues involved in self-harm than others, as well as the usual resource and time pressures endemic in the Prison Service. These practical steps can help keep the young person from being exposed to other prisoners' stares and possible taunts, and make the environment on the wing more manageable for them.

Psychotherapeutic workers may also find themselves dealing with young people who have been placed in segregation. Children and young people are placed in segregation units when they are deemed to be unmanageable or a risk to others on the wing. In practice this means that they often house the most disturbed and distressed children and young people, who respond to the control of their environment with violence, directed towards themselves or others. Although there have been legal rulings stating that juvenile offenders should not be placed in segregation units, they often are when they present a major management problem to the prison. As children, they should still have access to education; although once again the reality of an under-staffed, under-funded Prison Service means that this may occur on an ad hoc basis or not at all, leaving the child locked up for virtually the whole day. For children and young people who use self-harm to distract from unbearable thoughts or to reduce a physiological state of agitation, time on a segregation unit can be intolerable. They may try to find other methods to hurt themselves that they are not familiar with and are very likely to hurt themselves as soon as they return to the wing. For such young people a cycle of increased self-harm can ensue.

Segregation units form a major part of the disciplinary infrastructure of prisons. The regimes in the units are such that it is impossible to do any detailed confidential therapeutic work. However, it is possible to keep contact with the young person, find out what happened for them to be placed there, and to arrange a future date to meet. This continuity of contact can be crucially important to the young person. By organising a meeting soon after the young person's return to the wing, crucial support can be offered at a time that has been identified as high risk, and workers can help the individual to put in place structures or activities that make them feel safer. For example, they can ensure the young person has support 'chats' on request, with a member of staff they trust, or is able to attend a group they had previously been part of within the prison.

At a wider systemic level, workers who are in positions where they can input to the management of the prison are able to give advice on the suitability of the segregation unit for young people who are hurting themselves and argue for more suitable accommodation for them, for example, in a healthcare centre or a secure unit where they can receive more intensive specialist support.

DEALING WITH THE EMOTIONAL AND PSYCHOLOGICAL ENVIRONMENT

The small number of Young Offender Institutions in the country means that a young person may be located as much as one hundred miles from their family, making face-to-face contact extremely difficult. Even if families live nearer to the institutions, this is not always easily accessible; and getting there without a car can be problematic and time-consuming. This can lead to physical and emotional isolation for the young person.

In practical terms, workers can help with this situation by negotiating with prison staff to arrange additional phone calls to family. Sometimes family visits can be arranged by the Chaplaincy Service, depending on the particular prison establishment. In therapeutic sessions, giving young people time to talk about their family and friends and connect with them (through remembering) can be beneficial. It may be that a meeting with a counsellor or therapist is one of the few places in which they feel safe enough to do this. Workers can also help young people identify others within the prison who may be able to support them and who they feel safe with. These may be peers or staff. Sometimes the young person feels so unsafe around others that they do not feel making relationships is an option within the prison and prefer to be as solitary as possible on the wing. Helping the person to see that this is a positive choice they have made to look after themselves gives them a sense of control and a context to understand what they need at that time.

As discussed previously, the prison environment is hierarchical, with formal and informal practices of power. In this context, young people who deliberately hurt themselves are often seen as manipulative and attention-seeking. The consequences may be overt formal punishment such as segregation, loss of a job, or the person being placed on a 'basic' regime, with no television or personal effects for a limited period. Alongside these measures are the informal practices of power. These may, for example, take the form of healthcare staff refusing to clean wounds, so as not to 'encourage' attention-seeking. Young people may also be viewed as deliberately hurting themselves in order to be removed from the wing to healthcare for 'an easier life'. As a consequence, if placed temporarily in healthcare, they may be given little access to activities and limited time out of their cells, with the nursing regime taking a punitive, rather than rehabilitative position. The aim of these strategies is to return the individual to the wing as quickly as possible. It may well be appropriate for a young person to be returned to the wing. However, strategies of isolation, ignoring distress and removal of activities may have a converse effect. This is the case when they increase distress and thus increase the likelihood of self-harm when the opportunity arises. This usually occurs when the young person returns to the wing and may set up a cycle of self-harm that increases in severity over time. At this point, interventions such as group work for developing young people's coping strategies or communication skills and emotion management can be useful. Such groups have been established in Glen Parva and Wetherby Young Offenders Institutions with some success (Howard League, 2003). Development of these skills may prevent escalation of the young person's self-harm.

Repeated self-harming behaviours on the wing may lead to young people becoming marginalised and emotionally isolated from their peers. Furthermore, prison staff, who may previously have been supportive of the young person, may struggle to do so in the face of continued distress. Frequent self-harm tends to culminate in a decision to bring a young person off the wing and into a healthcare unit. This further establishes a pattern where the young person becomes dislocated from the main part of the prison. They have little contact with their peers on the wing, and may be viewed as a 'slasher' or 'psycho' by peers and some prison staff. They may lose their prison jobs and have limited access to education or group work in an attempt to restrict their access to methods of self-harm. Their television may also be taken to remove access to glass in their cell. They are left with little to occupy themselves. In addition, the regime of the prison healthcare system means that they are under constant supervision and frequently questioned about their self-harming behaviours. With little to distract them, and a persistent focus on why they hurt themselves, they can become locked into a specific identity focused around self-harm (Madigan, 1998).

Individual or group therapeutic work can provide a framework that explains the context of the prison and how the regime works, making explicit the formal and informal practices of control. This allows a young person to understand how and why the system responds to their self-harming behaviour, opening up the possibility of relating in a different way to the prison system. For example, if a young person cuts and puts razor blades in their mouth, they may well be removed from the wing and placed in healthcare, being unable to work or attend education. By helping the young person understand the prison's response and concern that further self-harm may occur, the young person can look at what he or she wants, hence providing them with some sense of control. If they want to get back to the wing what do they need to do? How do they convince the prison system that they are 'safe'? Such conversations might also include looking at how they self-harm once they return to the wing.

Children and young people who used self-harm in the community for several years are unlikely to stop immediately and will have developed a knowledge and experience of how it helps them survive and what methods help them harm 'safely'. The removal of their usual method of self-harm may lead them to resort to unfamiliar methods for example, self-ligation or hanging. This increases the risk of suicide because the young person does not know how far they need to go to inflict the degree of harm needed for physiological release or to gain a sense that they are coping emotionally and mentally. By discussing these issues with young people, workers not only provide education about the risks of different types of self-harm, but can also help them to find alternative yet safer ways to deal with their distress. Possible solutions may include not cutting so deeply, scratching rather than cutting, using alternative activities to distract themselves and encouraging the use of any available support services (such as befriending or listening schemes).

It could be argued that this encourages compliance to a regime that is often aggressive in its response to self-harm. It is a constant ethical tension for professionals but it can also be about trying to help a young person survive with the least possible distress in a hierarchical system. It is about helping the young person to understand that whilst they are in the prison they are subject to particular rules and practices and there are consequences if they don't adhere to them.

ESTABLISHING THERAPEUTIC SPACE AND CONVERSATIONS

Establishing space for young people to have these types of conversations is not always easy in a forensic setting. Yet probably one of the most crucial things a worker can do is to offer a young person a safe space to talk about what is going on for them, and what they think might help them. It is important that the young person themselves decides to see the professional or voluntary worker (rather than being told to see them by prison staff) and that this decision is an informed one. Initial meetings explaining what can be offered, and information leaflets, can be helpful at this point. A choice of whether the worker is female or male should be given, but if this is not possible, then exploring how this might influence working together is important. Many of the young people will have had difficult or abusive relationships and may not want to, or be able to, engage with someone of a particular gender.

Young people are very aware of how their responses are shared between staff and also how other prisoners within a healthcare unit or on the wing might overhear the conversations. This can exacerbate feelings of shame, anger and helplessness that may have led to the self-harm initially. Meeting with the young person in a quiet space and discussing what is happening for them and how confidentiality operates within the prison system involves them in the process. There needs to be a clear understanding of what has to be shared around risk and what remains confidential. By making these issues explicit, the young person is able to make a choice about what to share and what the consequences of sharing information will be.

If information about risk has to be disclosed to others then the young person may want to be involved in that process. Therapeutic workers can ask the young person if they would like to sit in on their conversation with the prison officer or healthcare nurse. This transparency of practice has the potential to set up a different power dynamic, in which the young person is not positioned as powerless and invisible. They are aware of the extent of the information that has been disclosed and the response of the prison. Once the limits of confidentiality have been established, therapists and counsellors can begin to work with the young person to break the psychological dislocation they are likely to be experiencing.

Social constructionist ideas of identity suggest that a person's sense of who they are is a product of the stories that are told about them and that they tell about themselves. These produce a familiarity and continuity for a young person, enabling them to recognise descriptions about themselves and how they behave in different contexts. The young person can also be quite fragile depending on the context in which they have grown up. Receiving a custodial sentence or remand order can shatter a young person's sense of their own past and also their future. They are positioned as 'prisoner' and 'criminal' (as well as a 'slasher'). Once in a prison setting young people are often cut off from the other stories that could inform their identity because they have little relevance in that particular setting. They have to try and forge a new identity to attempt to survive the prison system. This can be a time during which self-harm or attempted suicide increases, as the young person is in a state of 'not knowing' who they are or where they are going. Professionals can work with them to help them connect with parts of themselves that they have lost touch with in prison. This can be done with artwork or stories, or any medium that enables the person to access and hold on to a sense of herself or himself that has a future and feels more familiar. One young man I worked with reconnected with dancing, something he had loved doing outside. At night, alone in his cell he would dance. This gave him a strong connection to who he had been and also a sense that he had a future outside his immediate situation.

CONCLUSION

In summary, professionals and voluntary organisations can help young people in prison who self-harm by working with individuals, and also working to change things at a wider systemic level. They can explore with young people the context in which their self-harm occurred, how it helps them, and how they can manage it within the prison setting. Providing a framework of how the prison system works can help the young person negotiate ways of managing their self-harm within the limits of the prison, so that it does not escalate to the point of physical restraint. In my experience, the tensions of trying to work therapeutically within such a system remain ever present. Sometimes these tensions come to the fore and at other times they recede. However, if we do not work within these systems to influence reactions to young people who self-harm, not only do the myths around self-harm remain unchallenged, but, more importantly, no alternative ways of understanding or coping with distress are offered to young people in custody.

REFERENCES

Babiker, G & Arnold, L (1997) *The Language of Injury: Comprehending self-mutilation.* Leicester: The British Psychological Society.

Foucault, M (1977) *Discipline and Punish: The birth of the prison.* London: Penguin.

Godsi, E (2004) *Violence and Society: Making sense of madness and badness.* Ross-on-Wye: PCCS Books.

Golding, KS, Dent, HR, Nissim, R & Stott, L (2006) *Thinking Psychologically about Children who are Looked After and Adopted: Space for reflection.* Chichester: Wiley.

Howard League for Penal Reform (1999) *Desperate Measures: Prison suicides and their prevention.* London: Howard League for Penal Reform.

Howard League for Penal Reform (2001) *Repetitive Self-Harm among Women and Girls in Prison.* London: Howard League for Penal Reform.

Howard League for Penal Reform (2003) *Suicide and Self-Harm Prevention: The management of self-injury in prisons.* London: Howard League for Penal Reform.

Howard League for Penal Reform (2006) *Lord Carlisle's Inquiry into the Treatment of Children in Penal Custody.* London: Howard League for Penal Reform.

Madigan, S (1998) Inscription, description and deciphering chronic identities. In I Parker (ed) *Deconstructing psychotherapy* (pp. 150–63). London: Sage.

Mental Health Foundation (2002) *The Mental Health of Young Offenders. Bright futures: Working with vulnerable young people.* London: Mental Health Foundation.

NACRO (2003) *Counting the Cost: Reducing child imprisonment.* London: NACRO.

National Institute for Mental Health in England (2004) *National Suicide Prevention Strategy for England: Annual report on progress 2004.* London: NIHME.

Warren, D (1999) Setting new standards for foster care. *Adoption and Fostering, 23* (2), 48–56.

Chapter 11

HARM MINIMISATION:
LIMITING THE DAMAGE OF SELF-INJURY

Louise Roxanne Pembroke

MY OWN EXPERIENCE OF REALISING THE CONCEPT

As a teenager I knew nothing about first aid, anatomy, physiology or wound care; I didn't study science at O or A level. At 17, I attempted to kill myself and took a Paracetomol overdose believing I would fall unconscious and quietly die in my sleep, escaping the intolerable pain of living. Within months of my unsuccessful attempt I was injuring myself: initially superficial scratches, then the cuts became deeper.

Psychiatric hospitalisation only compounded my need to harm myself, and the response from staff was frequently angry and hostile. Back at home as my distress and isolation deepened, I would go to my local GP surgery with wounds but was frequently referred to Accident and Emergency (A&E). There, I learnt what good and bad care meant. One doctor would stitch wounds which extended to the bone of my arm with just a skin suture, not bothering to repair the underlying layers. As the verbal humiliation and hostility increased with each visit to A&E, I became increasingly reluctant to attend for fear of the response I would get.

At this point in my life I was struggling with reduced eyesight due to a rare eye condition, was too depressed to continue with a college course I had worked hard to get onto, and had very little in my life after psychiatric admissions. Friends were scared of the loony girl who was rumoured to be carving herself up. In short, I lost hope, and didn't think that anyone else believed in me either. Loss of hope jettisoned my need to self-injure. As I became more depressed by the responses to my self-harm this turned into what Gethin Morgan refers to as 'malignant alienation' (Morgan, 1993). I became increasingly alienated and withdrawn from everything to the point that I felt death was preferable to the responses my self-injuring generated. So I attempted to die again.

Not only did I not know how to look after myself, I didn't care to. My general state of health deteriorated, the ophthalmologist could see this in my eyes and I stopped going to A&E, but my inability to look after myself resulted in septicaemia. The Social Service day centre wouldn't accept me on grounds that I was too much of a danger to myself and my GP told me that I risked losing the use of my arm. He might as well have said that my head would drop off because I didn't understand *how* I could lose the use of a limb.

Ros was my ophthalmic nurse and had known me since I was 14 years old. She saw this bright outgoing girl turn into a slumped shadow of herself. She also grasped just how traumatised I was with the deterioration in my eyesight and how this must have impacted on someone who was in full-time dance training which requires good sight. Ros knew I was harming myself and during one appointment she asked 'What's wrong, are you hurt?' I said I was but that I couldn't face the humiliation of A&E. She calmly asked to see the wound. I was adamant there was no way I was going to A&E, even if I did get septicaemia again. So she offered to me help look after it so that it didn't happen. It was a bad wound, down to the bone again, which I didn't realise because I expected a bone to appear bright, shiny white. I didn't realise that bone is covered in a yellowish layer of connective tissue called periosteum.

Ros gave me my first lesson in anatomy and physiology when I was 18 years old. She explained what each layer of tissue was called, what its function was and what could happen to it if damaged. I learnt that the yellow globular stuff was *fat*, the purplish-brownish bit underneath which looked like meat at the supermarket was *muscle*. That the white cords that join the muscle to the bone were *tendons* and they were really something I didn't want to damage because *that's* what could have resulted in loss of mobility (now the GP's warnings made sense). I learnt the difference between veins and arteries and that it was easy to not see a nerve before cutting it. At least most of my serious injuries were *longitudinal*. This means there was less risk of cutting completely through tendons and it was easier to treat and medically repair. That afforded me slightly more safety, but had been luck and not judgement on my part.

Ros taught me how to recognise the symptoms of infection and how to minimise the risk of it occurring, such as by using clean blades, washing my hands, pulling the wound together with *steristrips* or tape and dressing it with appropriate dressings. Although wounds to the bone really should be repaired properly with each layer of tissue sewn together, she understood that at that point I couldn't face going to A&E and that it was more important to give me the necessary basic knowledge so that I didn't put my life or limb at risk.

This non-judgemental and practical approach was imparted without any lecturing or catastrophising and had a profound impact on me. Ros was the first person who didn't recoil in disgust or become angry, negative or distressed about my need to self-injure. She understood that was where I was at in my life and she *accepted* me whether I harmed or didn't harm. I didn't have to hide it, justify it, or make bargains or promises I couldn't keep. It was such a relief. I knew I could ask her for straightforward advice about any aspect of first aid and wound care.

For the first time I had some *control* over my circumstances. I had *choices*, I could *choose* to stop cutting at a certain point, I could *choose* to position the blade the other side of the vein to avoid a major bleed, I could *choose* to make it cleaner and safer. It might not seem like much of a choice but it is when you are striving to stay out of the psychiatric system, cope with extreme experiences and failing eyesight. It's a big deal. Having some physical control over my self-injury was my first step towards engaging more actively with the need to injure and negotiating with that need. It might be similar to intravenous drug users having access to clean needles, or good sexual health services not dictating abstinence to people having multiple sexual partners but, instead, promoting safer sex by the use of condoms to prevent the contraction of HIV. Some alcohol dependency services also address limiting the damage that can result from heavy alcohol consumption. These services have debated and practised the concept of *harm minimisation.*

Contrary to popular psychiatric myth that women 'grow out' of self-harm, for me the opposite was true. My worst self-injury occurred during my 30s. The following description might be difficult for some readers to look at as it describes in detail how harm minimisation can be also be applied to surgically serious self-injury.

I am a voice hearer; I hear voices both inside and outside of my head and some I can see and feel. One group of my voices are snakes and at times parts of my skin would be changed into snakeskin. I found this unbearable and the only way I could relieve my distress and halt the transformation from spreading was to remove the skin. This was quite a different form of self-injury and required a different approach to minimising the damage. I attached artery clips to the edges of the flap to be removed so that I could pull it back and see where I was cutting, as skin doesn't fall away from the body until it's a sizeable area and scar tissue makes it more rigid. I know this sounds horribly surgical but I didn't want major blood vessels to be severed by effectively cutting 'blind' with a blade under a flap. I couldn't get to hospital quickly. I understood the risks of applying a tourniquet, and I knew I would have been unable to call for an ambulance in those circumstances because I couldn't have placed enough value on myself to do so.

The use of artery clips with those injuries saved me from severing major blood vessels and worse damage than needing a skin graft to repair it.

THE CONCEPT OF HARM MINIMISATION:
APPLICATION AND PROMOTION

Harm minimisation is about accepting the need to self-harm as a valid method of survival until survival is possible by other means. This does not condone or encourage self-injury but is about facing the reality of maximising safety in the event of self-harm. If we are going to harm it is safer to do so with information on basic anatomy, physiology, first aid, wound care, correct usage of dressings and safer ways to harm. By 'safer' self-harm I'm referring to *how* we injure, *what* with, and *where*. The risks of harming with *no* information are far greater than the risks of harming *with* information. If we have no information we have no *choices*. Harm minimisation, the act of making injuring as safe as we can, in itself can result in a reduction of the severity or frequency of the harm, or at least help to prevent life- or limb-threatening damage. It promotes *thinking about* limiting the damage, *attempting compromises* with oneself, and prevention where that is possible. It promotes self-management, which is crucial in the area of self-harm, as many people do not find appropriate support within NHS services.

For some professionals, harm minimisation is not an acceptable idea if their only definition of progress or recovery is total cessation of the harm. I would argue that total cessation is not the only measure of progress; if we do less damage, take better care of ourselves, or feel better about ourselves, that can constitute progress too. In conversation with health professionals, a Dialectical Behaviour Therapy (DBT) trainer stated that 'a happy self-harmer is not progress'. However, I think they are missing the point. Recovery can mean learning to live with enduring and complex problems and developing a range of coping strategies, which, while they don't exclude self-harm, over time, with appropriate psychological and social support (as defined by the individual) can mean that self-harm is not the sole method of coping. This can then lead to cessation.

Harm minimisation is just *one* part of the equation. It is also important that both oneself and one's supporters accept the need to self-harm and try to develop an explanatory frame of reference to understand the origins, evolution, meanings and functions of our self-harm within the context of our life histories. Such an understanding should result in a range of strategies for survival that will reflect *our* definitions and experiences. Engaging with our distress means that we move from being managed by *others* to *self-management*.

DEVELOPING AND PROMOTING HARM MINIMISATION

Part of my journey from others trying to manage me to my own self-management led me to join with others who self-harmed. I became a founding member of National Self Harm Network (NSHN) and its first Chair (1994–2000). In this capacity I led a project to promote the concept of harm minimisation and organised two 'Risk Reduction' conferences in London and Manchester funded by MIND (NSHN, 2000). As a result of listening to members' experiences of dire treatment, notably, but not exclusively, within A&E Departments, we were acutely aware that poor treatment increased the risks of further self-harm, and increased the risk of poor wound management resulting in worse disfigurement.

The specific aim of the Risk Reduction conferences was to counteract the negative impact of poor treatment by enabling survivors to manage their own self-harm. This was a ground-breaking approach because nothing like this had been attempted before. It felt like a risk to do it, but we knew we had to! The conferences addressed a very wide range of issues from as many angles, involving as many experts-by-experience and professions. However, the conferences were only open to people with first hand experience of self-harm as we didn't want to get hooked into debating about the concept, we just wanted to get the information to the people. I am not suggesting that people who self-harm should *have* to look after their injuries, far from it, but I do believe that greater knowledge can decrease the risks of self-harm. In order to make this clear, I include a brief description of topics covered in the conferences.

The conferences started with a nurse and medical student who talked about anatomy and physiology in plain English with easy descriptions and clear anatomical drawings. They explained simply what structures looked like because in order to limit the damage you have to know what you're looking at! We talked through how and what damage can occur and difficulties with repairing some structures. This is because most people who self-injure don't actually have a desire to end up with reduced mobility. We detailed the principles of First Aid (specific to cuts and burns) and what to get for a First-Aid kit, along with wound care principles. We stressed the areas of the body to try and avoid, and safety points such as cutting along the direction that structures grow longitudinally to reduce the risk of cutting tendons. We looked at how the direction and the way cutting occurs, along with aftercare and dressings can influence *scar minimisation*. We looked at controlling blood loss and stopping burning along with assessing the damage and signposts for when to seek medical help.

Other areas we detailed included: recognising the signs of infection and further safety tips such as looking at what you're doing, slowing down, not harming whilst under the influence of drugs/alcohol, and sharper implements being safer than blunt ones because of the degree of pressure that has to be applied, especially with scar tissue which is much tougher.

We were very clear that harm minimisation principles *did not* apply to any internal damage such as overdoses because internal damage cannot be seen nor assessed except by medical testing at hospital. Likewise, the effects of *eating distress,* such as low potassium, cannot be assessed except by medical tests.

At one of the conferences a plastic surgeon talked about surgical procedures to reduce or change the appearance of scars, and at both events we had a Red Cross skin camouflage practitioner talk about, and demonstrate, this excellent free service available to anyone who is scarred. In the subsequent book we produced after the *Cutting the Risk* conferences, I added to the surgeon's contribution in a section about what to consider if seeking surgery for scars as this is not a straightforward issue (NSHN, 2000). It was gratifying to see the book reviewed by the British Journal of Plastic Surgery (Parry-Davies, 2000).

One member of NSHN gave an excellent talk about the psychological aspects of living and coping with scars. This took the conference into the more emotional side of harm minimisation. I was very much influenced by the work of the charity *Changing Faces*, which primarily works with people affected by facial differences and disfigurements. They assist people to feel proud of their appearance, to present confidently, and to manage effectively, negative responses from others. My idea of empowerment is that people would feel that they have the right to wear their skin however it looks.

The workshops during the conferences were truly inspiring. Participants came up with even more creative suggestions on a range of issues; practical, general, emotional and body image. In addition I include here some more examples taken from the workshops (NSHN, 2000). I must stress that we all experience different things as helpful or unhelpful and it depends on the context. This is not the definitive list of what people 'should' find helpful as we all need to find our *own* strategies and 'alternatives' which are unique to us. They are merely examples.

BEING PRACTICAL

Practical strategies included using cling film as a temporary dressing; using Friar's Balsam to help steristrips to adhere to the wound better; recognising the importance of substitution of different forms of harm to prevent greater harm; and keeping one body area free and sacrosanct (from injury). Emotional strategies included writing down your feelings on paper; feeling your feelings and trying to find support which acknowledges them; going through experiences in your head; and setting boundaries with others to help raise self-esteem. In relation to dealing with scars and body image, it seems important to encourage people to look at their body image as separate from their scars; create positive contact with our bodies (for example Indian henna painting) and developing strategies for scar visibility, for example going sleeveless in some places and having a cover for other, less safe situations. In addition, if people stare at our scars, we proposed that we could stare back! We also felt it was important to try and feel strong enough to hear of others harming less. Harm is just one facet of a person. Their identity is not just as a person who harms/doesn't harm.

These are strategies that people can do for themselves. However, there are also strategies which involve collaboration with others. For example, in the latter years of my worst self-injuring, my friend Dee Dee became my advocate, and what a wonderful advocate she was! With no experience or training she was naturally gifted in the art of not being threatening to staff but calmly assertive when necessary. She reassured me and made a difficult process as painless as it could be. Her presence removed an entire layer of anxiety from me so that I could concentrate on holding it together.

In order to invite services to be more collaborative there are a number of other practical strategies that can enable clinically appropriate and respectful treatment of self-harm. These include the provision of advocacy in A&E (see Bryant & Beckett, 2006), crisis cards, advance directives and consultant letters.

CONSULTANT LETTERS

Consultant letters are something really useful that psychiatrists can give their patients to take to A&E (or even better, get placed in their notes). This is pertinent to those with a long history of self-injury who are more likely to be subject to the worst excesses of medical and psychiatric violation. My previous consultant, Phil, drafted a letter for A&E/surgeons outlining just what I was having to deal with in my life and that negative approaches and traditional treatment made matters much worse for me. He suggested that the best thing they could do was to treat me according to clinical need, with dignity and respect, with the minimum fuss, and without any psychiatric dramas being imposed on me. Phil understood that when I harmed myself, the train had hit the buffers. He knew that I did everything I could to prevent that from occurring and that when it did happen, it really was my last option. He understood that psychiatric assessment made me feel homicidal and that even the slightest threat of admission could potentially result in attempted suicide, as he knew I would rather die than be medicated. Phil acted as my Monopoly *'Get out of jail free'* card.

CRISIS CARDS AND ADVANCE DIRECTIVES

Peter Campbell, a founder member of Survivors Speak Out, has spoken about, and campaigned for, both crisis cards and advance directives (Pembroke, 2006). Crisis cards came about as a grassroots idea launched at the Survivors Speak Out AGM in 1989. At the time of their introduction there were few, if any, advocacy projects so crisis cards were particularly important. Their prime purpose is to enable the bearer to nominate an advocate, but they also have room for short notes on what support the person most wants in a crisis. Crisis cards can be carried on the person and used in a mental health emergency, particularly if the individual is having trouble communicating. Some agencies have taken up the idea and added space for further information like details of people to contact, a person's GP and their medication. Crisis cards are a useful tool for outlining what helps/hinders and, if staff are open to this, it can make their jobs a lot easier and maybe more rewarding. Building on this, I have argued the case in the nursing press for advocacy services to be extended to A&E for people presenting with self-harm (Pembroke, 2000). I was also part of a research team that undertook the first study to explore the acceptability and practicality of such a service.

Advance statements are an extension of crisis cards. Advance statements enable service users to write down in advance what care and treatment they do (and don't) want. They can also include any information about themselves they want to tell mental health workers who may not know them well. Advance statements become particularly important if treatment decisions are being taken and the individual is deemed not to have the capacity to make such decisions. Advance statements are sometimes called 'advance directives', but currently we cannot force mental health workers to follow them as they are viewed as only advisory. It is hoped that advance statements will play a role in any new mental health legislation. I did successfully use an advance directive within a liver unit to prevent treatment that I did not want following self-harm.

I believe that consultant letters, crisis cards and advance directives can all be used to outline a person's preferred choice of injury repair, dressings and strategies for harm minimisation. These tools also aid communication and help enable the individual to remain more in control. Another useful strategy that some people have adopted is the use of direct payments. This is explored in the following chapter.

CONCLUSIONS

The Risk Reduction conferences and the resulting book *Cutting the Risk* were important milestones in the history of self-harm activism, not least because they were the first of their kind. Clearly the issue of harm minimisation remains important to people who self-harm and their supporters, as evidenced by *Cutting the Risk* being one of MIND's best-selling books. There is now increasing acceptance of the concept by mental health professionals and I think this helps to sideline the more unproductive interventions such as 'no self-harm contracts'. I would like to see A&E staff, practice nurses and mental health nurses joining survivor activists in using this in their work, as these professional groups are particularly well placed to do so. To facilitate this I recently organised the first harm-minimisation conference for health workers (Pavilion Publishing, 2006).

Can harm minimisation be done with young people or children? In my travels I've heard foster parents talk about doing so but obviously adapting the principles to the age group. As for teenagers and young adults—I think it is essential. I feel sad when I see young people with severe scarring or even reduced mobility caused by a lack of wound care. I look back to when I was a teenager and think how lucky I am to still have all my limbs intact; I'd like to think that future generations of young people who turn to self-harm will have more than luck on their side.

DEDICATION

I dedicate this chapter to my dear late friends Ros and Dee Dee.

REFERENCES

Bryant, L & Beckett, J (2006) *The Practicality and Acceptability of an Advocacy Service in the Emergency Department for People Attending following Self-Harm.* Leeds: University of Leeds, Academic Unit of Psychiatry & Behavioural Sciences.

Morgan, G (1993) *Malignant Alienation.* Speech at the Guild of Pastoral Psychology Summer Conference, 25th August.

NSHN (2000) *Cutting the Risk: Self-harm, self-care and risk reduction.* London: National Self Harm Network.

Parry-Davies, M (2000) Cutting the risk: Self-harm, self-care and risk reduction. *British Journal of Plastic Surgery, 54* (2), 185–6.

Pembroke, L (2000) Damage limitation. *Nursing Times, 96* (34), 34.

Pembroke, L (2006) Limiting the damage. *Mental Health Today,* April, 27–9.

Pavilion Publishing (2006) *Limiting the Damage: Practical harm minimisation for self-harm.* 24 November. ORT House Conference Centre, London.

Chapter 12

EXERCISING CHOICE AND CONTROL: INDEPENDENT LIVING, DIRECT PAYMENTS AND SELF-HARM

Helen Spandler and Pauline Heslop

INTRODUCTION

It is clear from other chapters in this book how crucial the exercise of power and control is to people who self-harm. For example, young people have been very clear that any support should respect their autonomy and not undermine their sense of control (Spandler, 1996). A consistent theme has been: how do we develop responses which support young people to remain in control whilst not merely condoning self-harm and effectively ignoring their pain and distress? One of the ways that self-harm survivors have begun to address this themselves is through direct payments, a funding mechanism based on the key tenets of choice and control. In the previous chapter Louise Pembroke argues that more mechanisms need to be developed which support survivors to work within their own understandings and frames of reference so they are able to *direct* their own support. The organisation 'Survivors Speak Out' is one of the few mental health organisations to have explicitly endorsed the expansion of direct payments to people who use mental health services. Therefore, this chapter explores the possibilities and limitations of using direct payments to facilitate greater choice and control, in relation to support around self-harm.

THE INDEPENDENT LIVING MOVEMENT AND DIRECT PAYMENTS

The 'direct payments' discussed here are *not* social security benefits paid straight into a person's bank account, but an alternative means of purchasing community care support. The idea of direct payments can be traced back to the early 1970s when young disabled people in the US forced their local authorities to give them the money that had been used to keep them in residential institutions (Glasby & Littlechild, 2002). With this money they employed their own personal assistants to support them to live their own lives outside of the institution and to go to college. Such action by disabled people laid the groundwork for the International Independent Living Movement (see Barnes, 1992; Kestenbaum, 1996; Hasler et al., 1999; Charlton, 1998).

The right to have individualised funding or direct payments to purchase one's own support and assistance is central to the Independent Living philosophy and has been campaigned for vigorously by disabled people (Campbell, 1998; Glasby & Littlechild, 2002; Hasler, 1999; Stainton & Boyce, 2002; Zarb & Evans, 1998; Evans, 2003). To the Independent Living Movement, independent living is not about people living alone and doing everything for themselves—unless that is their choice. Rather, it is about having choice about the personal support needed to ensure citizenship and social inclusion, with the support funded and provided in such a way that the individual, as far as possible, remains in control.

The 1996 Community Care (Direct Payments) Act (DoH, 1996) meant that service users assessed as eligible for statutory community care services (due to a range of disabilities including physical impairment, learning difficulties, and mental health support needs) can receive direct payments or individualised funding. This is a way of giving service users more control over their support arrangements by giving them the money with which to plan and purchase the support they think they need to meet their assessed social care needs. This enabled local authorities in England and Wales to offer adults receiving community care between the ages of 18–65 years the option of receiving the money instead of some, or all, of their support.

Since April 2003, it became mandatory for Local Authorities in England to offer direct payments as an option to everyone assessed as needing, or in receipt of, community care services. Direct payments have also been extended to 16–17 year olds (as well as older people and carers). The rationale for dropping the age limit was to gradually enable disabled young people to make more choices in their transition to adulthood (Morris, 1999). Although social services departments have a number of concerns about how younger people would manage direct payments, young people should not have to do this alone. It should be possible to utilise various supported decision initiatives pioneered in the learning disabilities field, such as user controlled trusts and circles of support (Heslop et al., 2001; Heslop, 2005). These are designated groups of people that the service user trusts to make decisions on their behalf, if they lack capacity, or feel unable to do so. They can include friends, family, advocates and/or workers. A Circle of Support is a non-professional group of supporters who have a strong commitment to an individual and helps them achieve their goals. A User Controlled Trust or Independent Living Trust is a more formal and legally binding groups of trustees who act on behalf of an individual or group of individuals.

So how might direct payments work in the mental health field? Currently the service user's 'care co-ordinator' (often a community psychiatric nurse or social worker in a Community Mental Health Team) carries out a community care assessment of need. Once assessed as needing a community care service, the service user should be offered the option of having some or all of their needs met using direct payments. With the resources paid directly to them, the service user can decide how they actually want to meet their assessed needs. To be able to negotiate and direct their own support and make decisions about what they need at a particular time has profound implications for people.

Such opportunities have led to recent initiatives promoting the use of direct payments in mental health (Davidson & Luckhurst, 2002, Heslop, 2001; Ridley & Jones, 2002). In 2001, a national pilot scheme was set up to increase awareness and take-up of direct payments by mental health service users across five local authority sites in England. The evaluation of this pilot scheme identified service users who were using direct payments to meet their mental health needs in a variety of creative and flexible ways outside the usual boundaries of service provision (Spandler & Vick, 2004). Follow-up work from the national pilot scheme has focused on enabling wider access to direct payments, including people from black and minoritised ethnic communities who are often believed to be underrepresented in take-up (Lowe & Newbigging, 2004).

Although there has been some concern that 'independent living' may be a Western concept which is alien to many cultures, this is often because of the misconception that it means living alone without support from family and community (Hasler et al., 1999). Others have argued that it is precisely because people can choose their own carers that makes it particularly suitable for many people from marginalised communities (Begum, 1995). This is especially the case given that service users should be able to choose to employ members of their own family or community (DoH, 2003). Of course it also enables people *not* to employ staff from within their own communities. It is often another assumption that people from minoritised communities always want workers that 'match' their ethnicity or cultural background, as if this were possible or necessarily desirable. (Chantler et al., 2001).

For the purposes of this chapter we focus on a small, but significant number of women who were using their payments to meet needs associated with self-harm. Although people may choose to meet their needs in a variety of ways through direct payments, employing and directing support workers or 'Personal Assistants' (PAs) has always been at the heart of independent living (Campbell, 1998; Glasby & Littlechild, 2002). For these women, using direct payments in this way has offered them a different perspective of choice and control than they might previously have encountered from mental health professionals.

USING DIRECT PAYMENTS

The concept of 'user control' might seem like a contradiction when considering meeting needs associated with self-harm. However many young people report that they use self-harm as a way of coping with intolerable distress when other coping mechanisms are beyond their control. By providing the person with the control to adopt other coping mechanisms, direct payments can, in effect, help the person control their self-harm. We offer some tentative examples to illustrate this point:

Janet,[1] for example, used direct payments to employ someone to stay with her during the night. Workers employed via direct payments are usually referred to as 'personal assistants' (PAs). Janet employed a worker for two waking night-sits per week when she felt she needed it most (for example at weekends). Janet had ongoing serious and escalating self-harm and suicide attempts, difficulties sleeping and would often feel acutely unsafe and vulnerable at night. Her PA would either help out with household chores while Janet slept, or sit up with her if she couldn't sleep.

> *It's very flexible. She comes in the evening and we have a drink and chat and take the dog for a walk sometimes and then I'll go to bed at whatever time and she might do some cleaning for me or whatever … then she sits up all night and when I get up during the night, I have got someone to talk to. That just gives me a chance to get some sleep, because I don't sleep very well, and I self-harm quite a lot … Just knowing that somebody is going to come in and spend the night and it gives me a bit of a break, somebody to talk to and I know I can phone her up too.*

According to both Janet and her social worker, this arrangement helped reduce the severity and amount of self-harm. In addition, she has had fewer hospital admissions; the admissions she had needed were voluntary, not compulsory, as had usually been the case; and when she had gone into hospital, she had been discharged sooner than previously because she had her support arrangements already in place. Janet managed to have an arrangement whereby her worker visited her in hospital and supported her on discharge.

> *[before this] I was spending a lot of time in hospital, I was in hospital for nearly half a year, every year, sometimes more … It's reduced it quite a lot. My PA comes to see me on the ward, she phoned a lot and kept in contact on the phone, she kept in contact with me, so the night I came home, she came that night too.*

---

1. Names have been altered to preserve anonymity.

In this way, direct payments were acting as a source of mental health maintenance and promotion to Janet, rather than merely being part of a crisis intervention process with a revolving door of entry to services.

Susan was looking at formalising a long-standing supportive relationship with a friend who she knew had sufficient knowledge and understanding about her situation and her self-harm.

> *I would say one of the biggest needs is to have someone understand why you are self-harming … If they know how that works they can also help you not do those things, or they can support you, if you do, in a way that's not patronising … To have someone that understands the reasons behind the self-harming, that makes a difference … Recently I self-harmed on my stomach and basically I didn't want to tell anybody and I ended up telling her and I had to go and see the doctor and then I had to go and see the nurse and I had lots of appointments, lots of dressings and she supported me all through that. She came with me to see the nurse, if the dressing fell off she learnt how to put the dressing on, she didn't criticise me or anything for what I had done to myself.*

For Susan, choosing a PA who understands self-harm and reacts to it in an acceptable way was crucial:

> *It would be awful to have someone as a personal assistant who said 'Don't do it', 'Why do you do it?' or 'That was a silly thing to do'. You know—those kinds of comments. She understands the reasons behind it and can talk about it afterwards, instead of criticising. We can have a sensible conversation afterwards. That does make a difference, because in the past I have had CPNs where I've just had loads of comments—you get that from the hospital anyway when you go and have stitches.*

Accounts by people who self-harm highlight the need for responses that are flexible, negotiable and open to change according to their varying needs at different times. This type of arrangement allows the service user to decide not only who, but also what, when and how they want to be supported and facilitates a more genuinely 'user-centred' approach. With this kind of arrangement the service user can draw up a contract with their PA identifying how they would like them to react and respond to their self-harm. For example, they may want to instigate a trial no-cutting rule at particular times with a view to finding alternative coping mechanisms, or they may wish to hold onto the option of self-harm whilst having the necessary support to enable them to continue to live their chosen lives. As Janet explained:

> *I've rung her before when I was thinking about [self-harming] and also afterwards. When I rang her afterwards she has come to be with me until I have gone to sleep, kept*

me safe ... On the other hand I've rung her before and said I really feel like it and she has come round and we have talked things out and I didn't harm myself. It depends on how you feel, what's happened in the day, on the circumstances really.

This whole process can give a whole new meaning to the term 'contracts'. People who self-harm frequently object to the setting of contracts which have been initiated by mental health professionals. In this arrangement, it is possible for the individual to draw up a contract with their PA on their own terms, either informally (verbally) or formally (written in job description or work guidelines). For example, Janet wrote a contract with her PA that she would not harm herself in her PA's presence, or during a specific period before or after her visit:

I don't do it while they are there, I wouldn't or I wouldn't normally do it before they come, and the day they come in either. I wouldn't do it in the morning if I knew they were going to come. Me and [social worker] come up with this together. If I feel like harming myself and she is due to come round then I'd tell her and talk to her about it instead. Sometimes I still feel like doing it but I can always talk to her about it.

Such contracts are very similar to forward planning tools such as 'Advanced Directives', sometimes called advanced statements or living wills (see Amering et al., 2005). These help ensure that, during a mental health crisis, service users retain control and choice. For example Linda recalled how she set out specific guidance to her PAs outlining how she wanted them to respond in a mental health crisis. She knew that when she was feeling extremely distressed and suicidal she would often refuse help, even when she desperately needed it. With this in mind she developed explicit guidance describing her personal signs of crisis (for example, refusing to answer the door) and outlining what the PA should do in such a situation. Advanced directives can also involve specific requests for help or 'advanced refusals' such as not wanting particular interventions or certain relatives to be informed.

Of course the PA would have to agree to these guidelines and should be able to discuss with the person concerned any problems with their implementation in practice. The whole process can help develop a useful dialogue between the service user and the PA as they negotiate their way through this. The kinds of arrangements described here, in order to work, may require a high level of self-knowledge and understanding. It is clearly not a particularly simple or straightforward process and requires careful consideration and the thinking through of any possible consequences. However, in doing this, it is possible for the person who self-harms to retain a greater level of control and can also help them to take on a greater level of responsibility over their behaviour and its emotional impact on others.

Such strategies build upon important work carried out by survivor organisations. They are a development from crisis cards and other survivor-led initiatives which have been advocated by organisations such as the Manic Depression Fellowship and Survivors Speak Out. In addition, they build on work done specifically by self-harm organisations. For example the National Self-Harm Network produced an information sheet designed for people who have self-harmed to use when attending an Accident and Emergency department. The information sheet provides a very practical set of questions that the person can respond to in advance about their injuries and how, specifically, they would (or would not) like to be treated. This was developed so that service users can, as far as possible, remain in control and retain their dignity and self-respect.

Using direct payments should not rule out the option of alternative approaches either instead of, or in conjunction with, direct payments e.g. more specifically psychotherapeutic interventions. Indeed, by providing them with the additional social support they require, some service users reported that direct payments could actually enable them to access and use psychotherapy. In this way, they could direct and manage their own support in ways that were consistent with, and complementary to, their therapy.

Some mental health service users also wanted to be able to use direct payments to purchase particular alternative therapies that are either unavailable on the NHS or deemed to be 'unsuitable' for their particular needs or diagnosis. At the moment direct payments can only be used for 'social' not 'health' care. Because these therapies are viewed as health interventions, it is not usually possible to purchase them with direct payments. However, this is currently being challenged by many advocates of independent living who want to see a wider variety of options available for service users seeking more holistic support.

TENSIONS AND DIFFICULTIES

Although direct payments offer a number of opportunities for service users who self-harm, it is certainly not the case of 'one size fits all': directly provided services have their place too. In reality, direct payments, as with any other service provision, can raise a whole new set of tensions and dilemmas, some of which are highlighted here.[2]

Firstly, choice and control are nebulous concepts and their exercise is limited by the personal, social, environmental and political contexts in which

---

2. A more general critical assessment of direct payments has been attempted elsewhere (Spandler, 2004).

they operate. Many service users' capacity for exercising choice and control has been undermined by their experience of mental distress and long-term use of mental health services. It might be a long and difficult learning process both for professionals, in giving up, and service users in taking on, more control. Not surprisingly, such difficulties can emerge most acutely when actually employing people. Then choices have to be made about who to employ, how and when a PA could best support the individual, and what guidelines the PA should be following. Greater 'choice' is often accompanied by responsibilities, constraints and consequences. The responsibility of being a 'good employer' and thinking through issues such as contracts, pay, insurance and back-up arrangements can be overwhelming—although every Local Authority should fund a support service whose role is to help service users with all of these issues.

Secondly, the use of direct payments may be constrained by the choices actually available, and possible, in a given social context. Service users need to be able to access direct payments in the first place. There is currently a high eligibility criteria for community care services, meaning that only people with 'severe and enduring' assessed mental health needs requiring statutory service intervention are likely to be able to access direct payments. Many people, especially young people, and people from black and minoritised ethnic communities may not use statutory mental health services, preferring voluntary community projects, precisely to avoid getting caught up in the statutory 'system'. During the National Pilot, it was evident that very few young people under 25 were accessing direct payments. Ideally, assessments should be needs-led and informed by self-assessment. However, in practice there are tensions between definitions and understandings of need, the assessment of which does not ultimately rest with the service user.

A further constraint is the quality of support possible through direct payments. If employing PAs, their ability to exercise choice and control relies heavily on the availability of workers willing to work for the relatively low wages that can be offered and prepared to work in often quite isolated conditions. The degree of flexible support possible can be dependent on finding people able to work at times necessary (often evenings and weekends) and usually for only a small number of hours each week. It also requires being able to find people willing and able to work and negotiate relationships in the ways that service users require. Self-harm can be very distressing both for the people harming themselves and for the people supporting them. The variety and complexity of tasks undertaken by PAs and their need to negotiate new ways of working requires a depth of responsibility and associated stress which should result in greater levels of pay, supervision and training than are generally provided for by direct payments.

There has been little focus on the presumably complex relationships and power dynamics between PAs and direct payment recipients. However, research carried out across disability groups found that, despite some problems, such relationships were usually mutually beneficial. Such relationships often made the negotiation of boundaries and responsibilities easier, contained important elements of trust, loyalty and affection and resulted in subtle shifts in power relationships (Glendinning et al., 2000). Despite this, the situation of PAs remains precarious as they often work alone, are low paid, un-unionised and may be dependent on the continued receipt of direct payments by their employer. Although this has been a concern for disability activists (see Ford & Shaw, 1992), it has not driven policy. Further research may be required to look at what support and supervision PAs might need, particularly in relation to supporting people who self-harm and/or attempt suicide which, as far as possible, ensures the service user remains in control. It may be possible for service users to direct their PAs to particular training and awareness-raising courses in relation to self-harm, like those run by local self-help groups and voluntary agencies such as 42nd Street and the Bristol Crisis Service for Women.

This discussion raises questions about the role of the voluntary sector in general. International research has demonstrated that, where governments promote individualised funding without resourcing community support networks in the non-profit sectors, the result can be a highly privatised system which limits the choice and control available to individuals without individualised funding (Lord & Hutchinson, 2003).

Independent living necessitates a shift in values and philosophy towards building greater capacity for choice and control and increasing client autonomy. More generally, it highlights the tension between maximising the potential for individual choice and control whilst maintaining a wider commitment to the collective provision of services. Direct payments have the potential of developing more creative and innovative ways of providing support and assistance (Torjman, 1996). However, people arranging their own support and funding on an individual basis has implications for the funding and availability of other collective support services. Therefore, a strategic approach to service development needs to balance two key elements. The first element is the structures in which individuals can articulate their claims for the support they need, such as advocacy services (Stainton, 2002). The second is the conditions which will support services that offer highly customised, specialised, publicly accountable and collective service provision and assistance to meet the changing and dynamic needs of groups and communities (O'Brien, 2001).

One way of resolving this tension is through the development of strategies which support the collective pooling of resources, such as the development of co-operatives. Co-operatives could give people more collective power in using direct payments. These could facilitate the expansion of community resources, the development of new communal services or the regeneration of services that have been run down (Ridley & Jones, 2002; Maglajlic et al., 2000). Co-operatives could be developed which help individuals to combine their payments to purchase care collectively and, if necessary, help recipients with employment and administration difficulties as well as providing a collective contingency or emergency fund. In the national pilot, for example, there was a group of service users who were using direct payments to buy in a creative arts worker (Spandler & Vick, 2004). The development of 'multi stakeholder' co-operatives has also been proposed, which would provide a structure through which direct payments recipients and PAs could openly discuss and negotiate key interests, have a powerful advocacy function, decrease individualisation and maximise the pressure for adequate resources (Lewis, 2002).

CONCLUSIONS

Although direct payments are not necessarily the best option for everyone, they do address many of the issues that are at the heart of demands of service users and survivors. Not all people who self-harm would be eligible for direct payments or would want to have them. However, some of the learning from the creative ways in which people are using direct payments could be built into existing service provision, and they do suggest alternative ways of managing the tensions so evident in current professional support for people who self-harm. Direct payments are not the only solution—nor are they a 'cure'. They are only as good as the support arrangements people are able to develop and negotiate. In other words, it is the quality of support possible through direct payments that is crucial rather than direct payments themselves. However, the use of direct payments is an important step forward in the provision of support for people who self-harm—provision that is generally not 'evidence-based' but based on past patterns of service provision or assumptions by professionals about what is needed. Service users who have pioneered the use of direct payments to cope with their self-harm have much that we can learn from in our efforts to work in a person-centred way that optimises choice and control.

Finally, we end on a cautionary note. Increasing powers to offer direct payments has been viewed as a victory by the Independent Living Movement. Direct payments are currently being promoted by government ministers and increased take-up is becoming part of the monitoring of individual local authorities' performance targets. This could offer service users increased opportunities for choice and control. However, direct payments must remain not only an option, but a *viable* one. Without investment in a wider supportive infrastructure necessary to enable service users to plan, direct and manage their own support arrangements, the principles of independent living at the heart of demands for direct payments could be compromised.

REFERENCES

Amering, M, Stastny, P & Hopper, K (2005) Psychiatric advanced directives: Qualitative study of informed deliberations by mental health service users. *British Journal of Psychiatry, 186*, 247–52.

Barnes, C (ed) (1992) *Making Our Own Choice: Independent living, personal assistance and disabled people*. Report of the BCODP Seminar on Independent Living and Personal Assistance, Herwood College, Coventry. Published (1993) London: Taylor & Francis.

Begum, N (1995) *Beyond Samosas and Reggae: A guide to developing services for black disabled people*. London: King's Fund.

Campbell, J (1998) From breakout to breakthrough: 25 years of legislative advocacy. In B Duncan & R Berman-Bieler (eds) *International Leadership Forum for Women with Disabilities: Final report*. New York: Rehabilitation International.

Chantler, K, Burman, E, Batsleer, J & Bashir, C (2001) *Attempted Suicide and Self-Harm (South Asian Women)*. Manchester Metropolitan University: Women's Studies Research Centre.

Charlton, JI (1998) *Nothing about Us without Us: Disability oppression and empowerment*. Berkeley: University of California Press.

Davidson, D & Luckhurst, L (2002) *Making Choices, Taking Control: Direct payments and mental health service users/survivors*. London: Joseph Rowntree Foundation/ National Centre for Independent Living.

Department of Health (1996) *Community Care (Direct Payments) Act*. London: Department of Health.

Department of Health (2003) *Direct Payments Guidance: Community Care, Services for Carers and Children's Services (Direct Payments) Guidance, England*. London: Department of Health.

Evans, J (2003) *Developments in Independent Living and Direct Payments in UK*. Presented at the European Network on Independent Living (ENIL) conference in Southampton, England, 7–9 March 2003. Internet publication <http://www.independentliving.org/docs6/evans200311.html>.

Ford, C & Shaw, R (1992) The user/personal assistance relationship. In C Barnes (ed) *Making Our Own Choice: Independent Living, Personal Assistance and Disabled People* Report of the BCODP Seminar on Independent Living and Personal Assistance, Herwood College, Coventry, August 1992. Published (1993) London: Taylor & Francis.

Glasby, J & Littlechild, B (2002) *Social Work and Direct Payments*. Bristol: Policy Press.

Glendinning, C, Halliwell, S, Jacobs, S, Rummery, K & Tyer, J (2000) New kinds of care, new kinds of relationships: How purchasing affects relationships in giving and receiving personal assistance. *Health and Social Care in the Community 8* (3), 201–11.

Hasler, F (1999) Exercising the right to freedom of choice. *Professional Social Work,* June, 6–7.

Hasler, F, Campbell J, & Zarb G, (1999) *Direct Routes to Independence: A guide to local authorities' implementation and management of direct payments.* London: Policy Studies Institute.

Heslop, P (2001) *Direct Payments for Mental Health Users/Survivors: A guide to some key issues.* London: National Centre for Independent Living.

Heslop, P (2005) Good practice in befriending services for people with learning difficulties. *British Journal of Learning Disabilities 33* (1), 27–33.

Heslop, P, Mallett, R, Simons, K & Ward, L (2001) *Bridging the Divide: The experiences of young people with learning difficulties and their families in transition.* University of Bristol: Norah Fry Research Centre.

Kestenbaum, A (1996) *Independent Living: A review.* York: Joseph Rowntree Foundation.

Laurance, J (2003) *Pure Madness: How fear drives the mental health system.* London: Routledge.

Lewis, F (2002) Co-ops and Community Living. Unpublished paper prepared by Fiona Lewis December 2002.

Lord, J & Hutchinson, P (2003) Individualised support and funding: Building blocks for capacity building and inclusion. *Disability and Society 18* (1), 71–86.

Lowe, J & Newbigging, K (2004) *New Directions: Direct payments and mental health.* London: Health and Social Care Advisory Service.

Maglajlic, R, Brandon, D & Given, D (2000) Making direct payments a choice: A report on the research findings. *Disability and Society 15* (1), 99–113.

Morris, J (1999) *Move On Up: Supporting young disabled people in their transition to adulthood.* Ilford: Barnardos.

O'Brien, J (2001) *Paying Customers are not enough: The dynamics of individualized funding.* Lithonia, GA: Responsive Systems Associates.

Ridley, J & Jones, L (2002) Direct what? The untapped potential of direct payments to mental health service users. *Disability and Society 18* (5), 643–58.

Spandler, H (1996) Who's Hurting Who? Young People, self-harm and suicide. Manchester: 42nd Street.

Spandler, H (2004) Friend or foe? Towards a critical assessment of direct payments. *Critical Social Policy 24* (2), 187–209.

Spandler, H & Vick, N (2004) *Direct Payments, Independent Living and Mental Health.* London: Health and Social Care Advisory Service.

Stainton, T (2002) Taking rights structurally: Disability, rights and social worker responses to direct payments. *British Journal of Social Work 32*, 751–63.

Stainton, T & Boyce, S (2002). I have got my freedom back: A report on an evaluation of direct payments in Cardiff and the Vale of Glamorgan. *Llais, 64*, 3–5.

Torjman, S (1996) *Dollars for Services: A.k.a. individualised funding.* Ontario: Caledon Institute of Social Policy.

Zarb, G & Evans, J (1998) What Price Independence? Paper presented at *Shaping our Futures,* A conference on Independent Living sponsored by the European Network on Independent Living (ENIL), London, June 1998.

FURTHER INFORMATION AND RESOURCES

• 42nd Street, Swan Buildings, 20 Swan Street, Manchester, M4 5JW, 0161 832 0170
www.fortysecondstreet.org.uk
42nd Street is a community mental health resource for young people under stress in Manchester. Useful resources and publications are available from 42nd Street including *In and Out of Harm's Way* by Alex.

• The Basement Project, PO Box 5, Abergavenny, NP7 5XW, 01873 856524
www.basementproject.co.uk
The Basement Project have produced many useful publications and resources for people who self-harm and/or have experienced abuse, including an educational resource pack about young people and self-harm and *The Self-Harm Help Book* by Lois Arnold and Ann Magill.

• Bristol Crisis Service for Women, PO BOX 654, Bristol, BS99 1XH, 0117 927 9600
www.users.zetnet.co.uk/bcsw/
Bristol Crisis Service for Women have written many useful booklets and publications about women and self-harm including booklets about supporting women from black and minority ethnic communities, self-harm self-help groups, supporting friends and family etc. including *The Rainbow Journal for Young People who Self-Injure*.

• MIND, The National Association for Mental Health, 0845 766 0163, www.mind.org.uk
Numerous useful publications are available from MIND including *Understanding Self-Harm* by Diane Harrison and *Cutting the Risk (Self-harm, self-care and risk reduction)* by the National Self Harm Network.

• National Self Harm Network, PO Box 7264, Nottingham, NG1 6WJ, www.nshn.co.uk
Publications include the *Hurt Yourself Less Workbook* and *Cutting the Risk (Self-harm, self-care and risk reduction)*.

• Working to Recovery Ltd, 4 The Beehives, Kimany Road, Wormit, Fife, Scotland, DD6 8PD
01382 542517, www.workingtorecovery.co.uk
Publications available such as *Working with Self-Harm: Victim to victor* by Mike Smith and *Killing me Softly: Self-harm survival not suicide* by Sharon Lefevre.

• Asylum, Limbrick Centre, Limbrick Road, Sheffield, S6 2PE, www.asylumonline.net
Asylum is an international magazine for democratic psychiatry, psychology, education and community development; Asylum Associates is a training, conference and publishing resource.

Other Useful Websites
• Young Minds (for children's mental health), www.youngminds.org.uk

• Mental Health Foundation, www.mentalhealth.org.uk

• www.selfharm.org.uk

• www.selfinjury.org

• www.self-injury-abuse-trauma-directory.info

NOTES ON CONTRIBUTORS

ROSE CAMERON

Rose was born in Scotland, near Inverness, and now lives in Manchester, where she has been in independent practice since 1993, and works as an external supervisor for 42nd Street. She is particularly interested in using insights from the current wealth of research in child development, neuroscience and other disciplines, to promote a better understanding of why people self-harm and what is likely to be most helpful.

DOUG FEERY

Doug is a barrister and works within the Mental Health and Human Rights Law areas. He now works in-house with Peter Edwards Law Solicitors, a leading mental health and human rights law practice. Doug covers two main types of work: the representation of patients at Mental Health Review Tribunals, and litigation cases. He is also currently progressing a number of important legal test cases around compensation payments for seclusion, unlawful detention and failure to provide single-sex inpatient provision.

THERES FICKL

Theres works as an individual and couples counsellor, supervisor and trainer at Counselling Initiative in Manchester. She has 16 years' experience in residential support work in various countries, using different theoretical approaches with a variety of age groups.

Prior to going into private practice she worked for the Manchester Project/Richmond Fellowship, a supported housing project for women who are survivors of sexual abuse. It was in this context that she made contact with 42nd Street in order to help young women build a supportive network. She also works as a trainer for Manchester Rape Crisis.

KEITH GREEN

Keith worked in mental health services for fourteen years—eight of those with 42nd Street's Suicide and Self-Harm Project. He currently works in the Community Arts field.

PAULINE HESLOP

Pauline is a mental health service user who has received direct payments for over five years. She currently works part-time as a researcher at the University of Bristol and provides consultancy/training on various aspects of mental health. Pauline has also worked with the National Centre for Independent Living (NCIL), and the West of England Centre for Inclusive Living (WECIL) in promoting the use of direct payments for people with mental health support needs. She is the author of the booklet *Direct Payments for Mental Health Service Users/Survivors* published by NCIL.

EAMONN KIRK

Eamonn has had numerous work incarnations, including sales assistant, cleaner at a psychiatric hospital, biology student, copy-editor and proofreader, CAB adviser, mental health support worker, social work student, suicide and self-harm worker. He was a Community Mental Health Worker for 42nd Street's Inside Out project, collaborating with young people who define as lesbian, gay, bisexual, or are questioning their sexuality. He is often labelled as white, gay, male, British/Irish, but doesn't strongly identify as any of these anymore. He enjoys creative writing, painting, cycling, playing the piano, hanging out with his partner and friends, and not cutting his hair.

VERA MARTINS

Vera is the Director of 42nd Street with over 20 years' experience of working with children, young people and their families. She strives to ensure that services targeting young people are rights-based and proactive in placing the young person at the centre. Respecting and engaging with issues of equality and diversity is more than a sound bite, as Vera says, it is her survival.

CAROLYN McQUEEN

Carolyn is a clinical psychologist who has worked with young people and adults in a variety of settings, including a young offenders institution. She is interested in how young people make sense of their lives and what works for them. She currently works as a Therapy Service Manager for an independent fostering agency in the Midlands.

Ian Murray

Belfast man, Ian Murray, started his training as a psychiatric nurse in 1971. He trained as a general nurse, a social worker and a community psychiatric nurse. In 1979 Ian worked in Lisburn as Officer in Charge of a community psychiatric hostel based on a large housing estate. As a lone resident worker, Ian worked for nine years, living with service users and raising his own family. In 1993, Ian commissioned and managed the award winning Dryll y Car unit near Barmouth in Wales where, supported by psychiatrist Phil Thomas, the staff evolved a more supportive approach in working with people who self-harm. Currently a CPN, Ian has written many articles on mental health.

Louise Roxanne Pembroke

Louise has been a psychiatric survivor activist for the last 20 years. She is a creative campaigner in the areas of self-harm, hearing voices and eating distress, former Chair of Survivors Speak Out and a founding member and the first Chair of the National Self Harm Network. Louise is the co-editor and co-author of a number of ground-breaking publications including *Self-Harm; Perspectives from personal experience* (1994, Survivors Speak Out) *The Hurt Yourself Less Workbook* (1998, NSHN) and *Cutting the Risk* (2000, NSHN). Outside of activism, Louise loves Star Trek, Dr Who and Bharatanatyam.

Gillian Proctor

Gillian is a clinical psychologist with North Bradford PCT mental health team and an honorary research fellow at the Centre for Citizenship and Community Mental Health at the University of Bradford. Ethics, politics and power are her special interests and publications include: author of *The Dynamics of Power in Counselling and Psychotherapy* (2002, PCCS Books), co-editor of *Encountering Feminism* (2004, PCCS Books) and co-editor of *Politicizing the Person-Centred Approach* (2006, PCCS Books). She has recently managed the setting up of a new pilot service providing medical treatment for self-injury in local GP surgeries in North Bradford.

Clare Shaw

Clare's own experiences of mental health services motivated her to become involved in the service user/survivor movement. She was a founder member of STEPS (a self-help group for women who self-injure) and Mad Women (a radical campaigning group for women with an interest in mental health). She is currently active in Women at the Margins, a Leeds-based group with a focus on borderline personality disorder. She co-formed Harm-ed, a training partnership providing training about self-injury, with Terri Shaw. Clare is also a poet and has been described by the Arvon Foundation as 'one of Britain's most powerful and dynamic young poets'. Her first collection, *Straight Ahead*, was published by Bloodaxe in 2006.

Terri Shaw

Terri lives in Burnley with her two children. Her youngest child has Down's Syndrome and it was when he was born that she decided to take a break from her career in nursing and venture back into the world of academia. Initially completing a degree in Nursing, she then did an MA in Bioethics and Medical Law. Her MA gave her the opportunity to research harm minimisation and self-injury. She has presented her findings at several national events and has also had several opportunities to speak from the perspective of a 'carer'—which is slowly beginning to gain some much-needed recognition. She co-founded Harm-ed with Clare Shaw.

Helen Spandler

Helen works as a Research Fellow in the Department of Social Work at the University of Central Lancashire. She has worked for a number of mental health organisations, including 42nd Street where she researched *Who's Hurting Who?* (1996, 42nd Street). She has also recently published *Asylum to Action: Paddington Day Hospital, therapeutic communities and beyond* (2006, JKP), a book about the history of a libertarian therapeutic community.

Sam Warner

Sam works as a freelance consultant clinical psychologist, trainer, therapist, and expert witness, and is a half-time Research Fellow at Manchester Metropolitan University. She specialises in work around child sexual abuse, within community and secure care services with children, adolescents, (and their parents) and adults. She has written *Understanding Women and Child Sexual Abuse: Feminist revolutions in theory, research and practice*, (in press) Psychology Press . Sam is also designing a training manual and producing a video pack (together with Flexible Films) for working with clients who have experienced child sexual abuse.

INDEX